SOCCER

PRESSING

JUST AFTER BALL LOSS

CONCEPT AND 50 DRILLS FOR TRAINING

Manuel Jesús Crespo García

©Copyright: Manuel Jesús Crespo García
©Copyright: De la presente Edición, Año 2021 WANCEULEN EDITORIAL

Title: SOCCER: PRESSING JUST AFTER BALL LOSS. CONCEPT AND 50 DRILLS FOR TRAINING
Author: MANUEL JESÚS CRESPO GARCÍA
Text correction: MANUELA CASTILLO SOLER

Publisher: WANCEULEN EDITORIAL
Collection: WANCEULEN EDITORIAL DEPORTIVA

ISBN (Paper – Color Edition): 978-84-18831-88-1
ISBN (Ebook): 978-84-18831-89-8
ISBN (Paper Black & White Edition): 978-84-18831-90-4

Legal deposit: SE 1486-2021

Printed in Spain.

WANCEULEN S.L.
C/ Cristo del Desamparo y Abandono, 56 - 41006 Sevilla
Web: www.wanceuleneditorial.com y www.wanceulen.com
Email: info@wanceuleneditorial.com

All rights reserved. It is forbidden to reproduce this work. No parts may be reproduced, stored or be transmitted in any form or by any means, electronic, mechanic, photocopying, recording of otherwise without written permission of the owners of the intellectual property.

INDEX OF CONTENTS

INTRODUCTION 7
CONCEPT OF **PRESSING JUST AFTER BALL LOSS** 9
SYMBOLOGY 15
50 DRILLS FOR TRAINING 17

INTRODUCTION

In the initiation to the world of soccer training, it is very common to try to find a formula that solves our needs, and that covers the possible gaps that we have in our knowledge.

Soccer is evolving, and new concepts with diverse interpretations are appearing, attending to the different currents to which we are most related. However, I think that everything can be adapted and can be profited, as long as you have a good argument and we do not allow ourselves to be drawn to dogmas.

The intention of this book is to manage resources, adapt them to our reality and that they can guide us to achieve our objectives in training.

I have reduced the use of material, in order to be able to reach any level of resources, without the need for materials that make it difficult to carry out.

There are different types of tasks to improve the collective domain of any medium that we want our team to handle during the development of the matches. Depending on the methodology used, the duration, spaces, number of players … can vary to satisfy our game model.

Next, I will develop different tasks from the simplest to the most complex to be able to work on the concept of pressure after the ball is lost, and which can be part of different game models. According to the claims of each coach and according to the methodology to be used, each one must introduce them how they consider appropriate.

Castellano and Casamichana (2016) propose this table for the classification of tasks, according to the square meters per player and according to the demands.

m² / player	1<2	3<4	5<7	8<10
<50	Strength		Recuperation	
<100				
<200	Heart rate		Speed	
>200				

In each drill the number of players, the division and distribution of the spaces will be indicated. However, in order for the task to be adapted to each team, the physical state of the players, the game model and the methodology, each coach must adapt the distances, the spaces and even the number of players in some cases, to have better development with the team.

The tasks will not have limits of contact with the ball to achieve our goal, since there will be players who use a greater number due to the needs of the game, technical conditions or physical conditions. However, as they are open tasks, the coach will be able to condition them if he deems it necessary, to achieve the intended benefits, knowing the reality to which he will expose them.

CONCEPT OF PRESSING JUST AFTER BALL LOSS

In the creation or development of the game models devised by the coaches, one of the options that can be taken is the pressing just after losing the ball.

González, A. speaks to us in his book: *Fútbol. La dinámica del juego desde la perspectiva de las transiciones,* in 2013, that the pressure-defense "consists of limiting the rival's ability to act, cutting off his initiative trying to quickly recover the ball" (...) "usually seeking recovery in the area where he lost it "(...)" will usually be done after loss "

This type of pressure or this moment in which it is "decided" to press, is usually identified with teams that want to take the initiative in the game with the ball, and who try to recover the ball as soon as possible.

The ball can be lost in several ways:

- The opponent retrieves it during the game.
- The ball remains 50-50s and can be taken by one team or another.
- Committing a foul, in which the referee stops the game, and determines that the opponent kicks.
- The ball leaves the field of play being my team the last to touch it and, therefore, the rival will put it into play.

The use of pressing just after losing the ball, must occur at the moment when the opponent recovers it, or when it is 50-50s, the ball is in play and there is an intention to dispute it.

To improve "pressing just after loss", the player's response when losing the ball must be automated. The indicators that must be assimilated to start the pressure mechanisms must be:

• I don't have the ball, the rival does.

• I don't have the ball, it's 50-50

Any other period of time in which a loss occurs, will be other more reflective moments in which you can press, but accommodating the players in the most suitable positions to perform them, not conditioned by the place they occupied while attacking (they had the ball).

Pressure is the action carried out when a team does not have the ball, over the rival, in order to restrict their freedom of action in space and time, induce them to take the ball to an area and cause the loss of the ball.

The pressure, from the point of view of who performs it, can be:

- Individual. Performed by a single player.
- Collective. It is performed by a group of players, or all players.

We can say that the "pressing just after losing" is a way to face, as a team, the moment when we lose the ball and it is still in play, being able to be carried out by all the players, by a group of them or by a single player, depending on the game strategy and on the team's game model, and according to the objectives we want to achieve with it. It is closely related to the attack-defense transition.

The objectives that we can achieve with "pressing just after losing the ball", are:

- Recover the ball.
- Prevent the rival from advancing towards our goal.
- Temporize.
- Maintain advanced positions.
- Defend ourselves from a position far from our goalkeeper.
- Not having to run backwards.
- Prevent the rival from crossing lines.
- Make it difficult to start the construction of the opponent's attack and, therefore, reduce the opponent's decision-making time.
- Avoid the rival counterattack.
- Prevent the opponent from deploying in attack.
- That the ball stays in the zone we want.

- Remain in a better situation for the attack, if we recover the ball.

The pressure after loss can also be selective in terms of the places or times in which to carry it out, depending on the game model and the structures used by one team or another. There may be a team that always faces loss with a defensive fallback and only performs "pressing just after losing" if the loss occurs at the beginning of the play from their own box and with the team deployed, for example.

Soriano, E. (2013) says that "We must understand that pressing just after losing the ball is a very risky action, which should only be carried out when it benefits us. That aggressive attitude if it does not carry a previous control, a balance, is a huge risk."

"Positional play" applies "pressing just after losing" as the first option when the ball is lost. The idea of having the ball, conditions an intense attitude to recover it when it is lost.

The concept of "pressing just after losing" is not the exclusive property of "position play". It can be used in any other situation, or at any other time considered appropriate, to favor a certain model.

"The way you manage the ball, indicates how you can collectively intervene when you don't have it" (Conde, M. 2010).

Each team can adapt it to obtain some benefit. This example of analysis by Eric Soriano (2013) of the "pressing just after losing" carried out by Fútbol Club Barcelona, clarifies how the team did it:

Pressing just after losing the ball in FCB		
Pressure on the opponent who has the ball	**Bring the lines closer to each other**	**Watch over "weak side"**
• Prevent the opponent from thinking and finding a pass option. • Orient the rival towards the areas that interest us. • Rival with the ball and backward, perfect time to press.	• Prevent the pass to nearby players. • Reduce spaces for pass	• Control of rivals away from the ball • Rational occupation to be able to shift after a long pass

(The Tactical Room, 2013)

Players need to know how, when, where, why and who to "press just after losing". We will use training to learn and master it. Poorly executed "Pressing just after losing" can lead to:

√ Leave spaces behind.
√ Enable the opponent's counterattack.
√ Being misplaced to participate in the game.
√ The opponent can strike in attack.
√ The opponent will assume the initiative of the game.

Players must be focused, activated quickly and with the appropriate intensity, at the moment they lose the ball. With effort attitude and good communication in the team.

Many authors speak of harassment, as the means to use for a good "pressing just after losing", to condition the opponent or to steal the ball. Other authors believe that you shouldn't harass your rival, but rather make them "feel pressured".

It is important that the player positions himself defensively with a balanced posture that conditions the rival to achieve the objectives of the "pressing just after losing", that he does not commit infractions (fouls), and does not rush, so as not to be easily overcome. As coaches we have to focus on giving the player feedback that the player understands, not giving him a long theoretical exposition. The idea is that the player, in training, thinks and achieves learning.

The stimuli to start the "pressing just after losing" will be stimuli of the game itself, to clearly identify the moment to carry it out. Pressing after an auditory stimulus (coach's voice, whistle ...) will help us to improve the reaction speed, but not the specific one of the medium or principle of "pressing just after losing".

SIMBOLOGY

Player	● 4
Ball displacement	⟶
Player displacement	┄┄┄►

PRESSING JUST AFTER BALL LOSS

50
DRILLS FOR TRAINING

SOCCER: PRESSING JUST AFTER BALL LOSS

Drill 1	Main Objective	Improving pressing just after loss
	Number of players	2

Explanation

The players pass the ball in pairs and when one decides to control, the other presses to steal the ball.

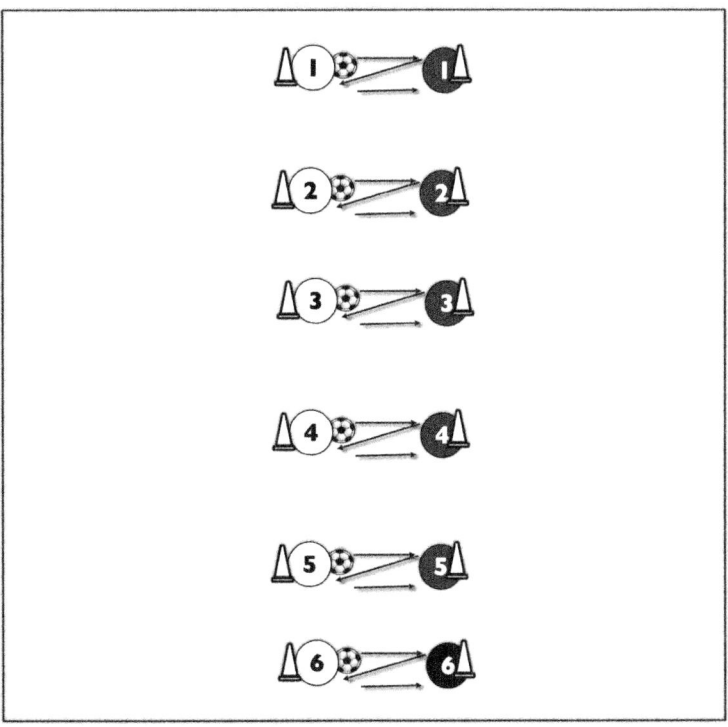

Drill 2	Main Objective	Improving pressing just after loss
	Number of players	2

Explanation

The players pass the ball in pairs without it falling to the ground, and when one falls the other player has to press to retrieve it.

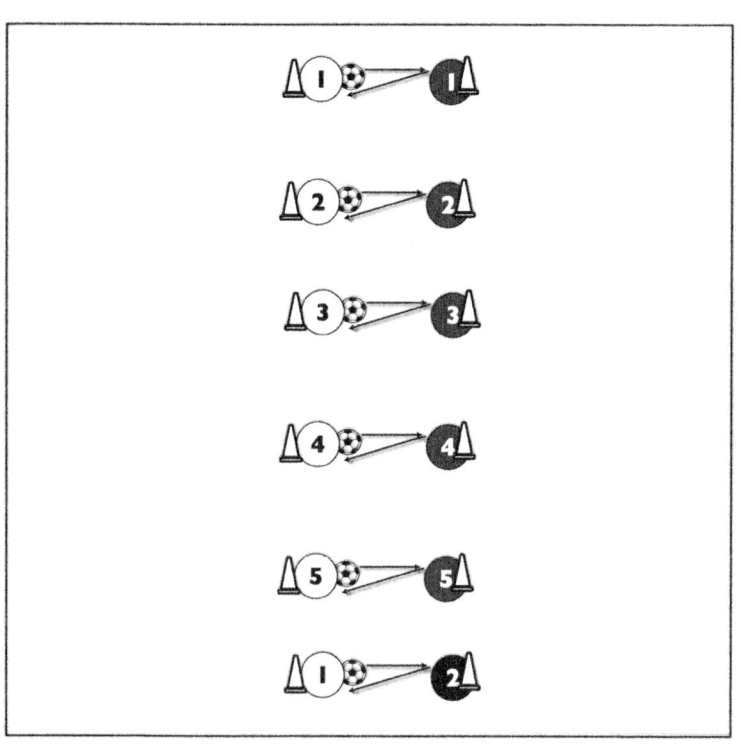

Drill 3	Main Objective	Improving pressing just after loss
	Number of players	4 (2x1+P)

Explanation

2 players pass the ball between them from the lines placed as in the image, and the central player tries to take it away. When they lose the ball, they will quickly press towards the center player who stole it. The central player will try to shoot at goal.

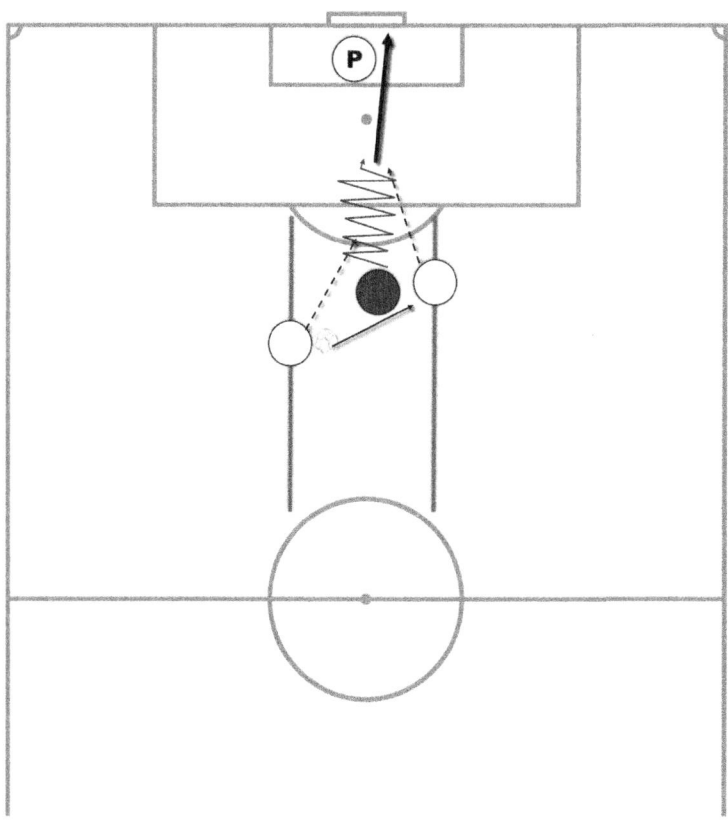

Drill 4	Main Objective	Improving pressing just after loss
	Number of players	2

Explanation

In pairs. Each player is touching the ball in the air without leaving the square. When a player drops the ball, or the ball leaves the square, the player goes to his partner to steal his ball.

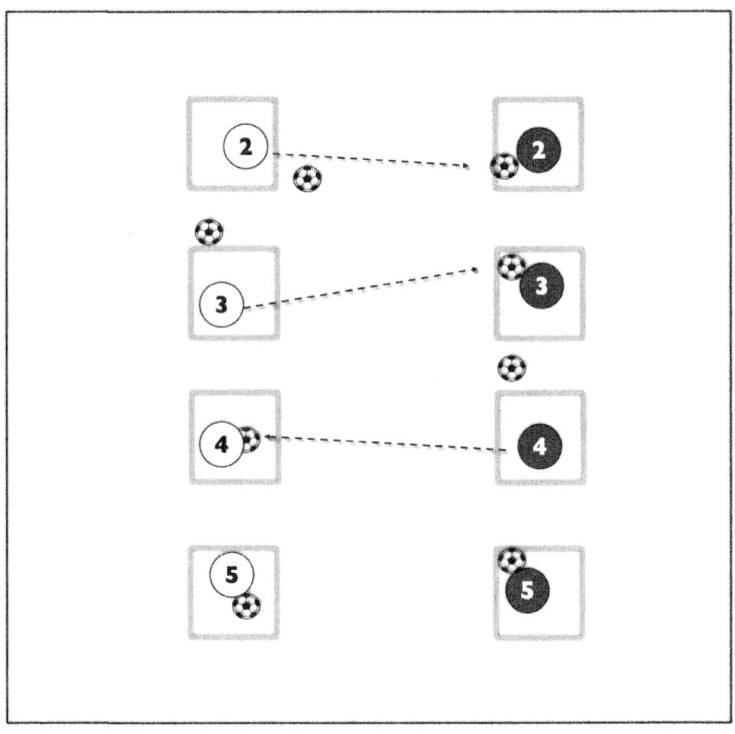

SOCCER: PRESSING JUST AFTER BALL LOSS

Drill 5	Main Objective	Improving pressing just after loss
	Number of players	2

Explanation

The players pass the ball in pairs, each in a square separated by a space, if when controlling the ball it leaves the square, the players have to compete to enter, with the ball controlled, in the square in front, where it is ek the partner (in which the partner was).

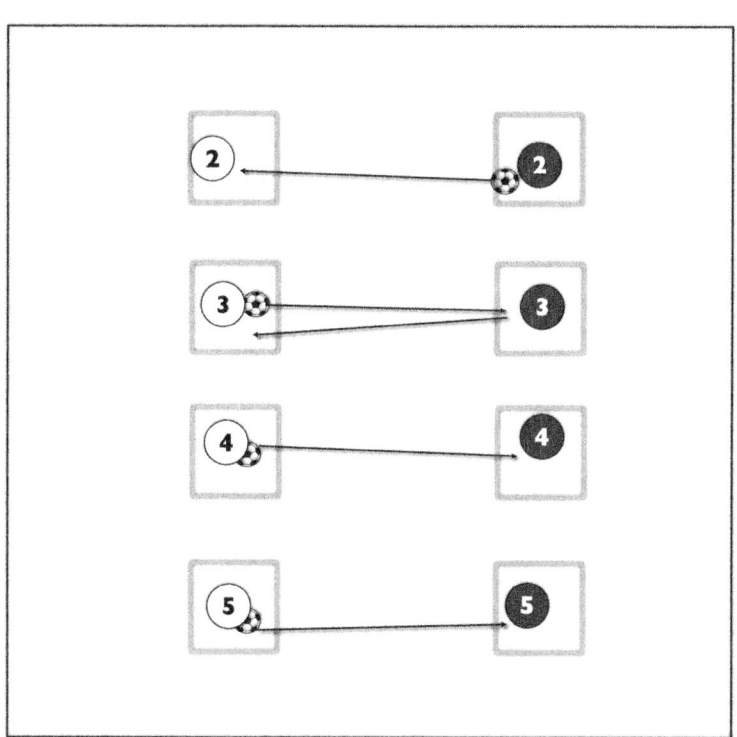

Drill 6	Main Objective	Improving pressing just after loss
	Number of players	3

Explanation

Players placed as in the image. They play 2x1 in a square and when the ball is stolen the one who lost tries to recover the ball, and the one who recovered it plays with the other player.

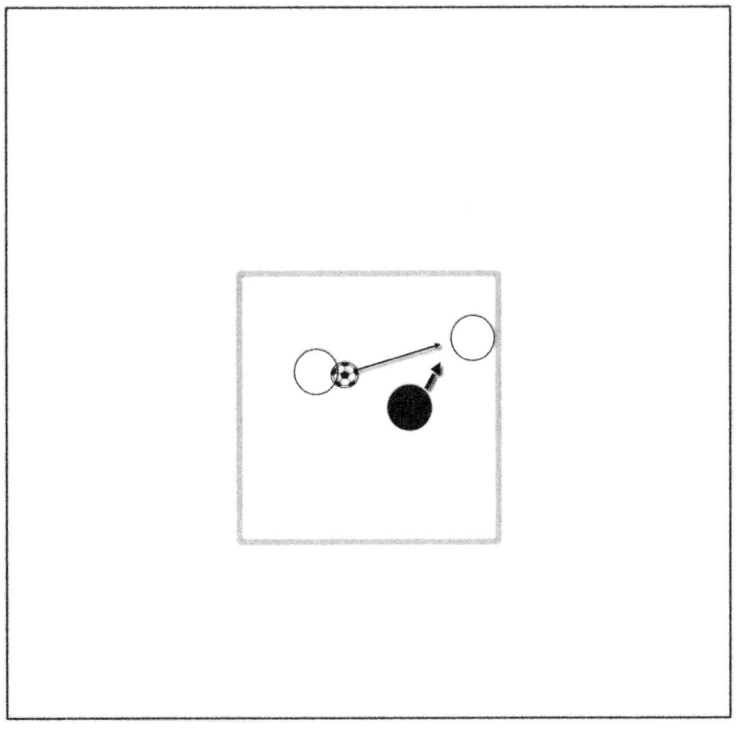

SOCCER: PRESSING JUST AFTER BALL LOSS

Drill 7	Main Objective	Improving pressing just after loss
	Number of players	3

Explanation

Players placed as in the image. They play 2x1 in a square and when the ball is stolen the two players who had it press the one who stole so that he does not leave the square with the ball, and to continue passing the ball.

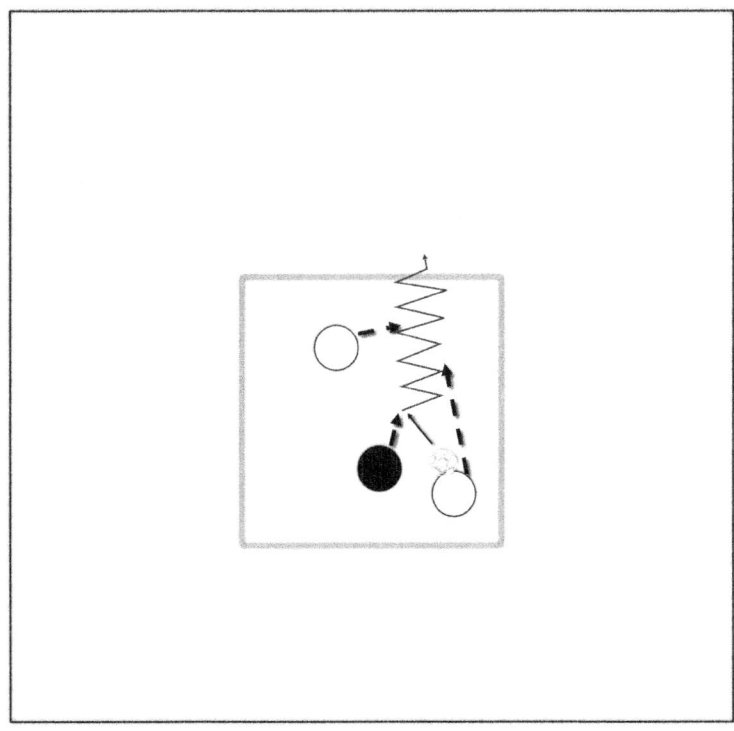

Drill 8	Main Objective	Improving pressing just after loss
	Number of players	7

Explanation

The possessing team (white) passes the ball aided by the joker in two squares, according to the arrangement of the image. The team without a ball (black) presses and is left with a player in the center who can go to help press any of the squares. When the white team loses the ball, it will press, and it will be the black team that maintains possession of the ball with the help of the wild card.

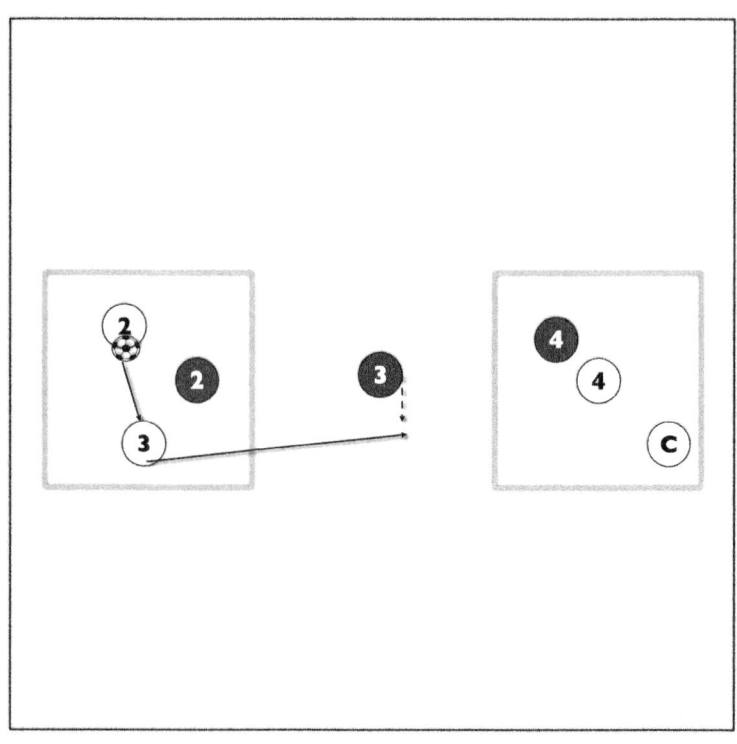

SOCCER: PRESSING JUST AFTER BALL LOSS

Drill 9	Main Objective	Improving pressing just after loss
	Number of players	16

Explanation

Players placed as in the image. In each square 7 players from each team with a ball each, and a player from the other team without ball, and trying to steal the ball from a rival player. The player who steals the ball goes to the other square to press and try to steal another ball.

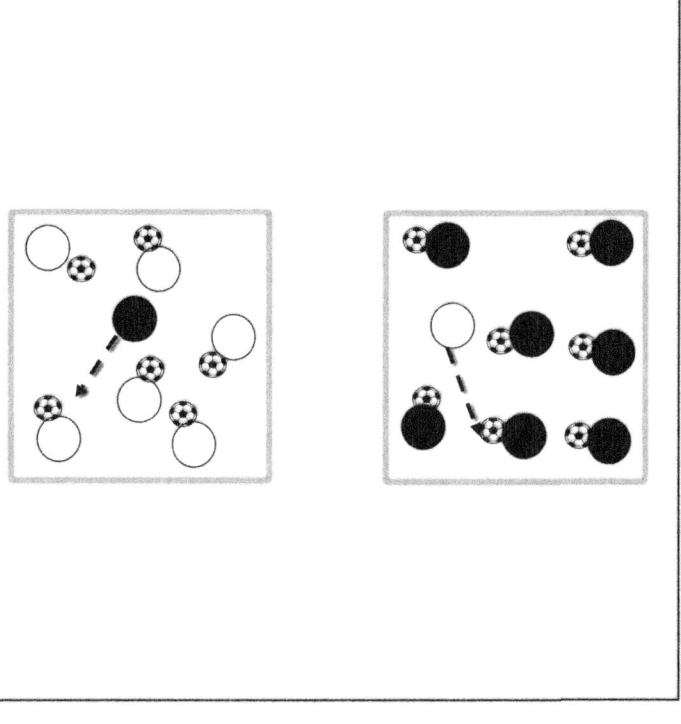

EDITORIAL WANCEULEN

Drill 10	Main Objective	Improving pressing just after loss
	Number of players	16

Explanation

Players placed as in the image. In each square 7 players from each team with a ball each. There are two outside the squares who pass the ball with their heads and, when they drop the ball, they go to the other team's square and put pressure on the opponents and try to get the balls out of the square.

The player who steals the ball presses the one who stole it to retrieve the ball before he takes it out of the box, if he takes it out he will have to leave it. The color that first takes the rivals from the square will win.

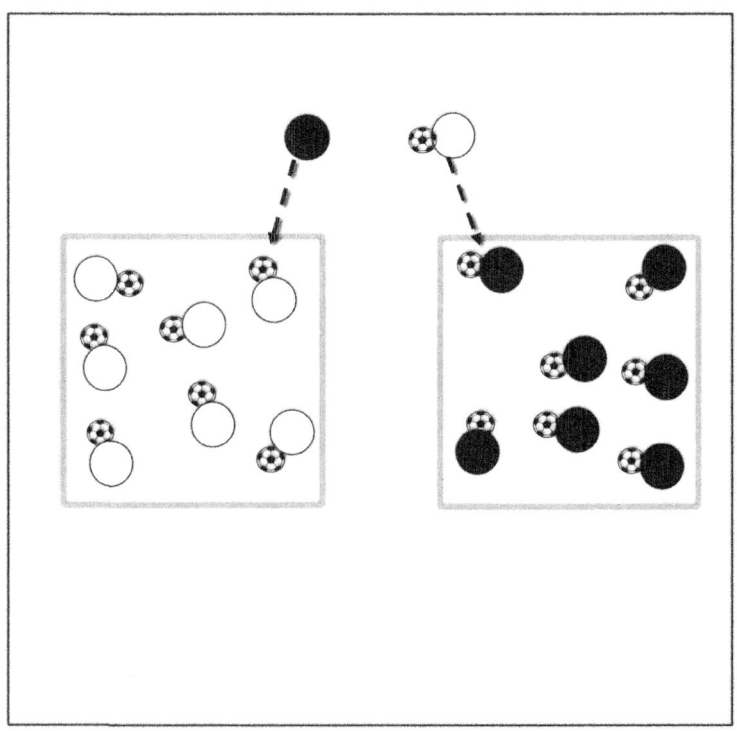

Drill 11	Main Objective	Improving pressing just after loss
	Number of players	19

Explanation

Players who have the ball have to cross to the back area. Those who do not have a ball will press to steal when the players who have a ball reach the center. The player whose ball is stolen may press another player.

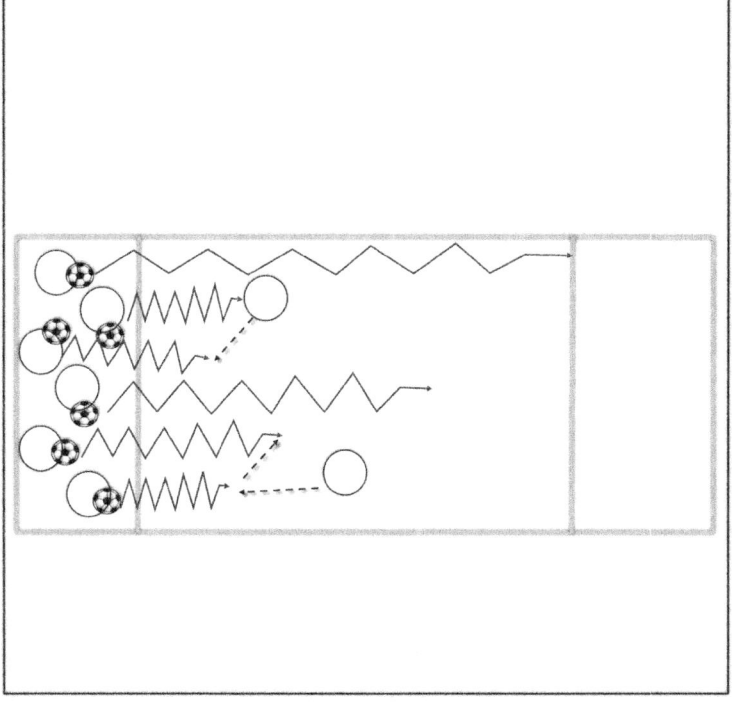

Drill	Main Objective	Improving pressing just after loss
12	Number of players	8

Explanation

Players who have the ball have to cross to the back area. Those who do not have a ball wait en the central zone and will press to steal when the players who have a ball reach the center. The player whose ball is stolen may press another player.

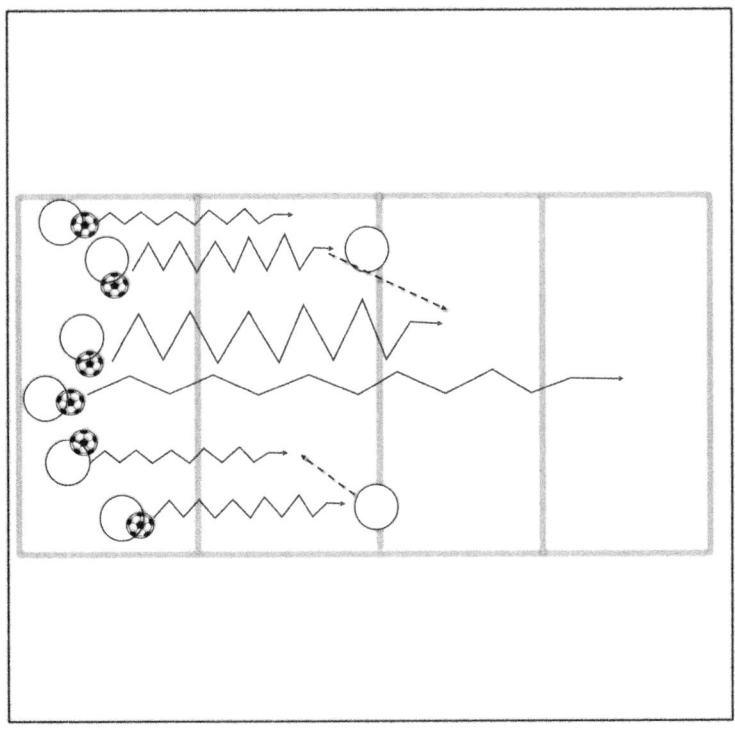

SOCCER: PRESSING JUST AFTER BALL LOSS

Drill 13	Main Objective	Improving pressing just after loss
	Number of players	19
Explanation			

Within the marked area the players pass the ball in pairs, and 5 players attempt to intercept the passes. When a player intercepts a pass, the player who passed the ball changes the role with the player who intercepted, and will have to go to intercept another pass.

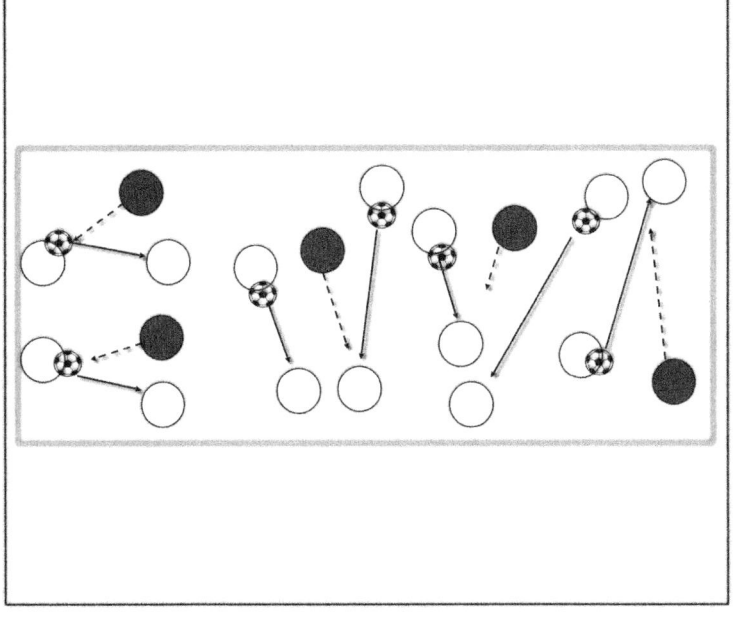

Drill 14	Main Objective	Improving pressing just after loss
	Number of players	11

Explanation

8 players in the rectangle drive the ball and there are 2 players without the ball who press to steal. When they lose the ball they have to press to steal fast. Those two players who steal quickly go out with their ball towards the goal, throw and return to the rectangle with the ball.

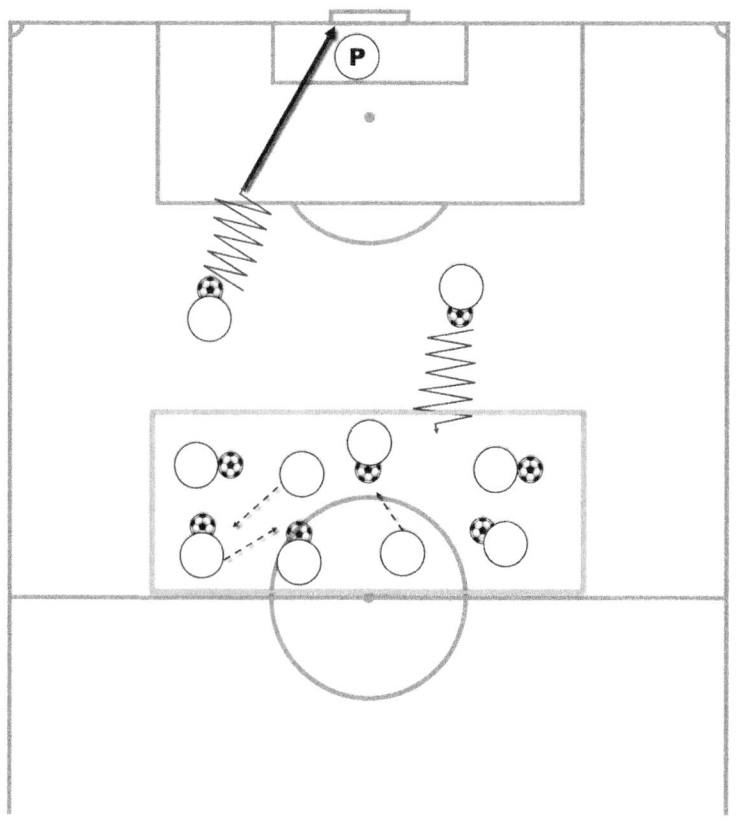

SOCCER: PRESSING JUST AFTER BALL LOSS

Drill 15	Main Objective	Improving pressing just after loss
	Number of players	20
Explanation		

Within the large triangle the players pass the ball in pairs, and 4 players press them to steal the ball. When a player steals a ball, the last player to touch the ball and lose it goes to the small triangle to press to try to steal a ball from another player. That player who loses it will go to the greater triangle to put pressure on a couple to try to steal the ball.

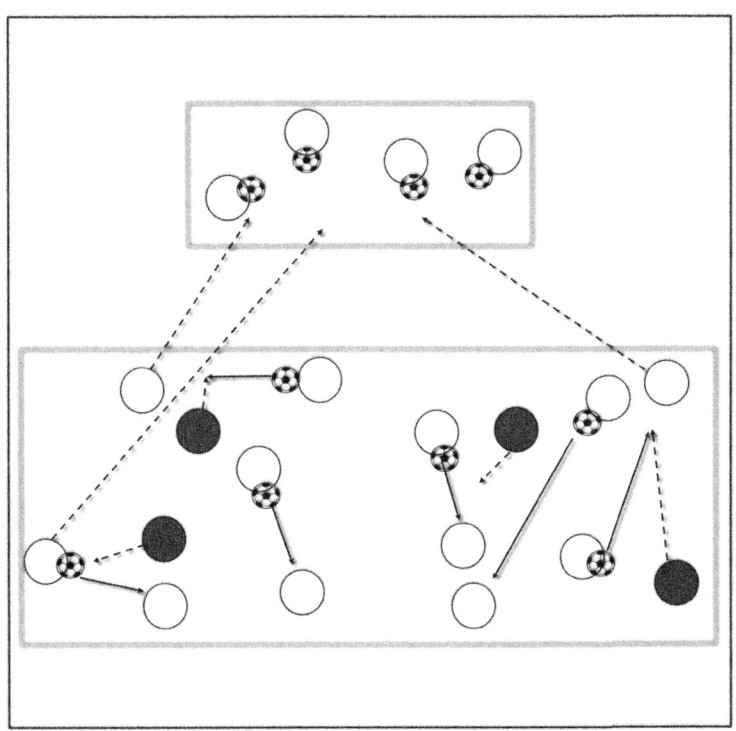

EDITORIAL WANCEULEN

Drill 16	Main Objective	Improving pressing just after loss
	Number of players	20

Explanation

Inside the area will be all the players with the ball, except 5 who will try to press to steal a ball. When it is stolen, the one who had the ball stolen will have to steal from another player, and the one who stole will try to keep it.

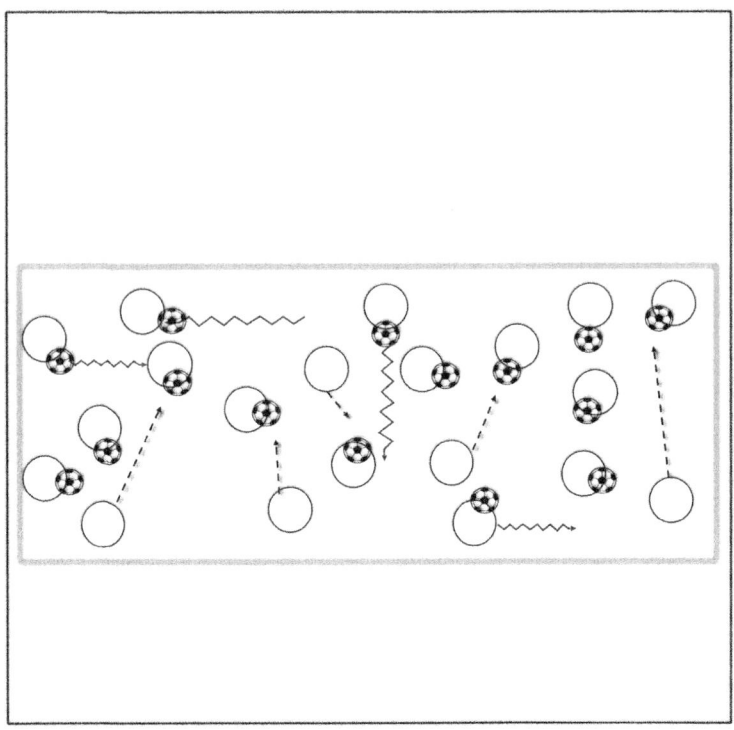

SOCCER: PRESSING JUST AFTER BALL LOSS

Drill 17	Main Objective	Improving pressing just after loss
	Number of players	15 (6+3x6)

Explanation

In a hexagon 6 + 3 against 6 is played in the arrangement of the image. Those who have the ball and are on the outside pass the ball along with those in the center (black team) and the remaining 7 (white team) try to anticipate or intercept the ball. If the white team steals the ball, the black team will press to retrieve the ball.

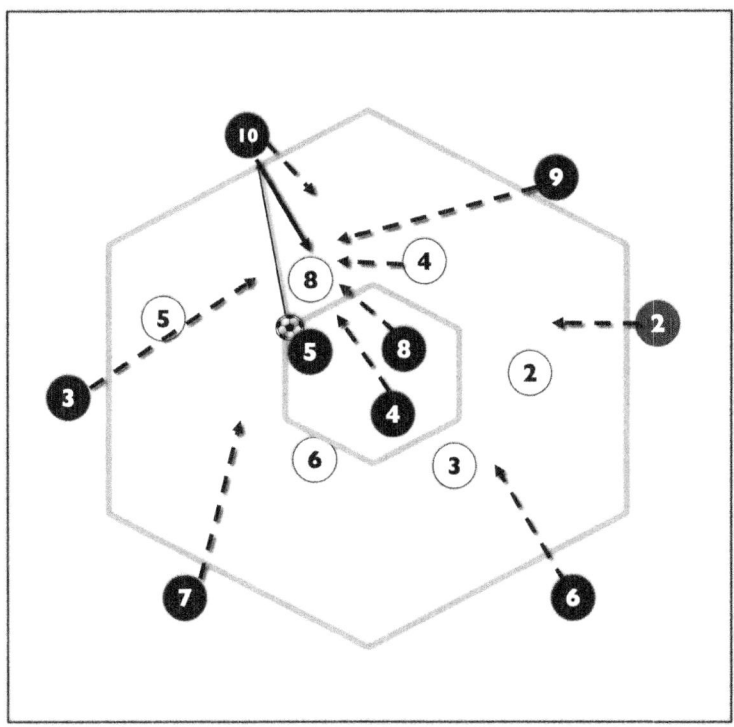

Drill 18	Main Objective	Improving pressing just after loss
	Number of players	10 (5x5)

Explanation

The players of the white team are distributed in the square: 4 in the corners and one inside. They pass the ball, the black team tries to steal, being able to move freely around the square. When the white team loses the ball, it presses and tries to retrieve it, to return to its positions.

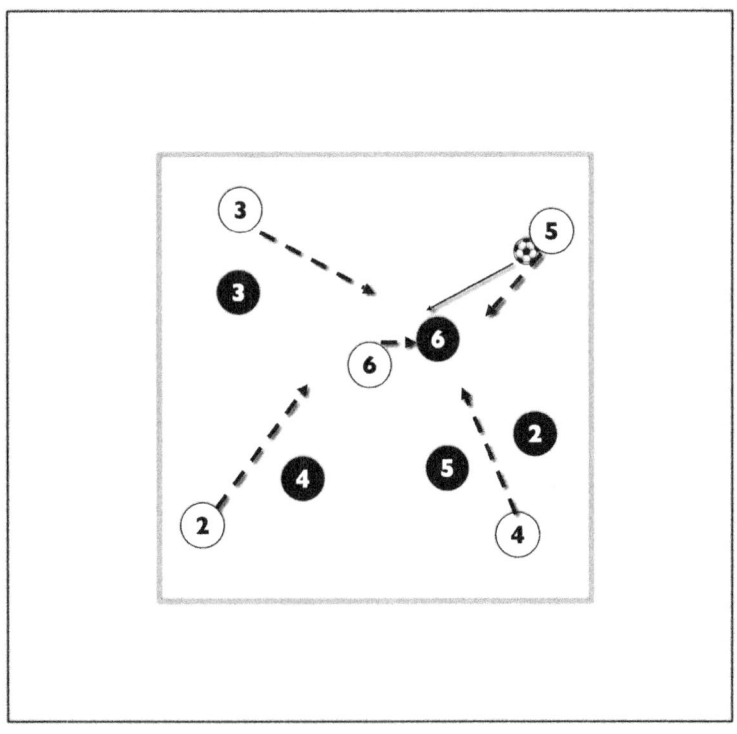

Drill 19	Main Objective	Improving pressing just after loss
	Number of players	10 (5x5)

Explanation

They play 5x5 with one to one defense. When they lose the ball they must each press their one.

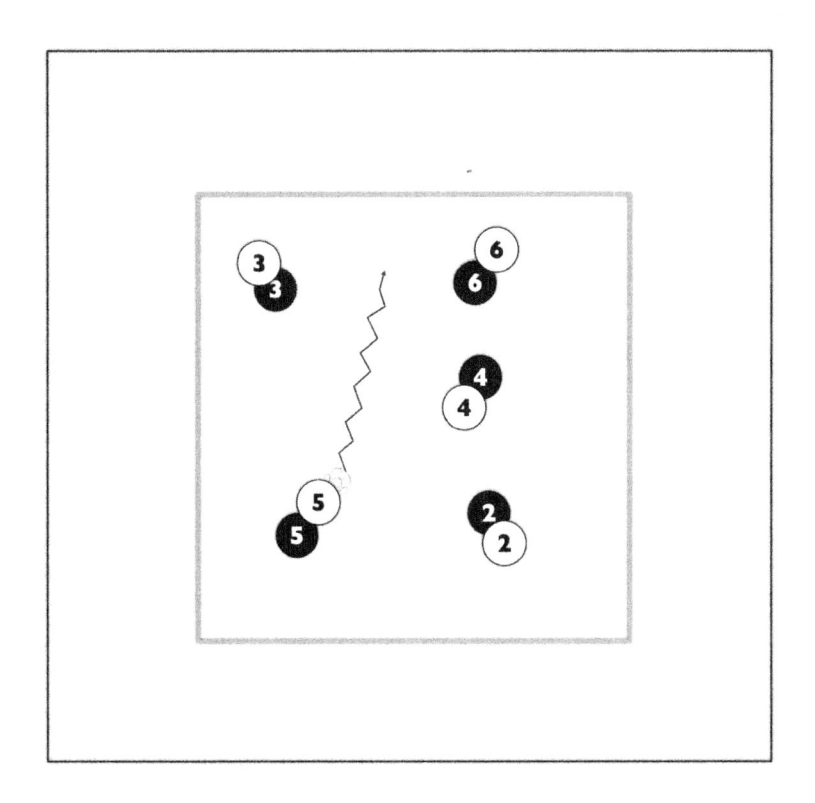

Drill 20	Main Objective	Improving pressing just after loss
	Number of players	10 (5x5)

Explanation

The players of the white team are distributed: 4 in the areas on the sides of the square, and one inside the square; the ball is passed between the 5. The black team tries to steal, being able to move freely around the square. When the white team loses the ball, it presses and tries to retrieve it to return to its positions.

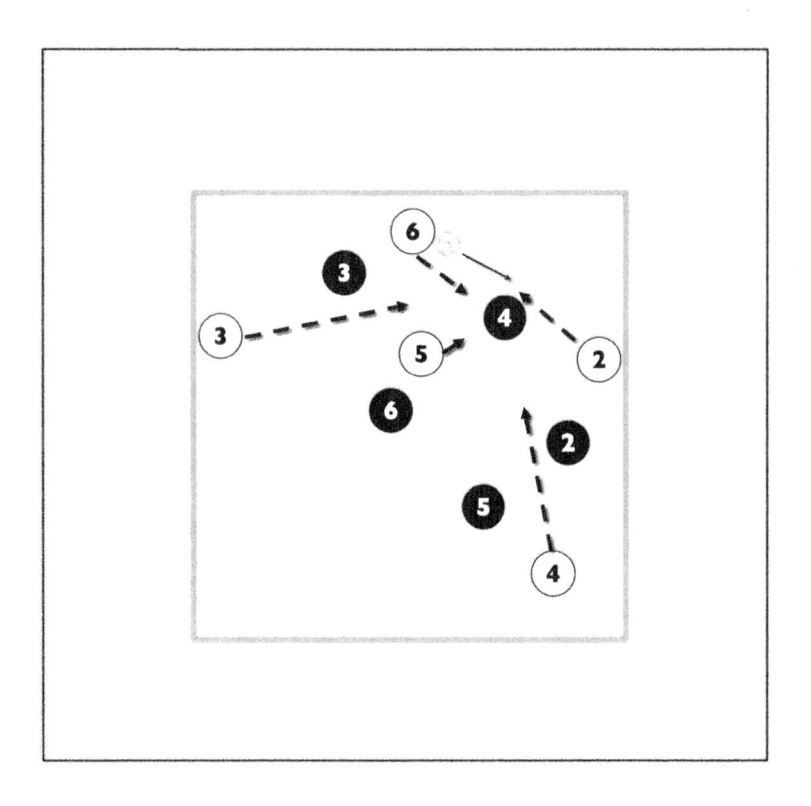

SOCCER: PRESSING JUST AFTER BALL LOSS

Drill 21	Main Objective	Improving pressing just after loss
	Number of players	14 (7x7)

Explanation

The white team tries to keep possession of the ball inside the square. The black team tries to steal the ball and, when it does, the white team will press to retrieve the ball before all the players in the team that stole it leave the square.

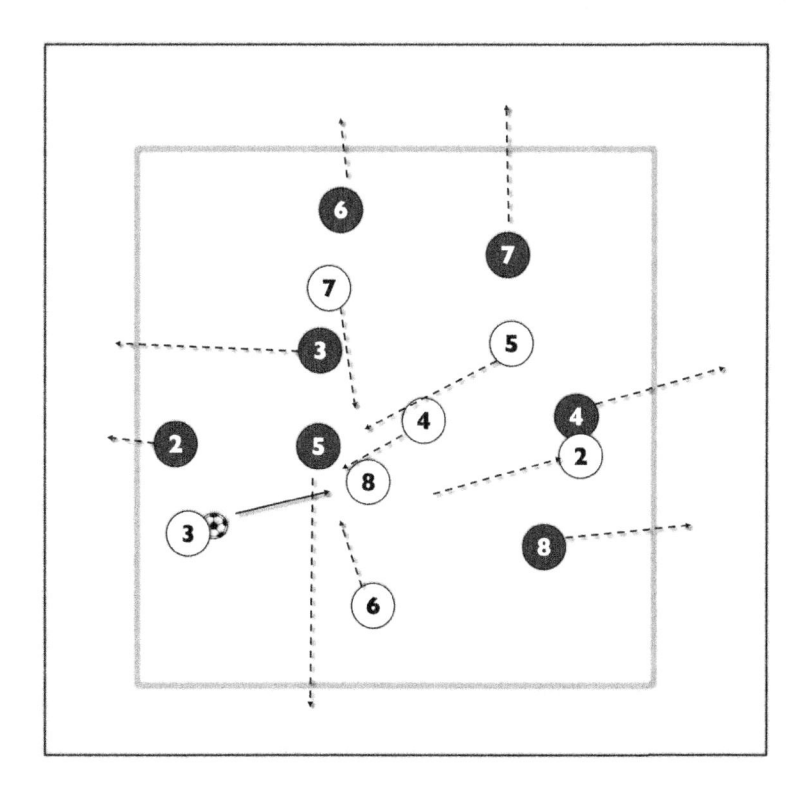

Drill 22	Main Objective	Improving pressing just after loss
	Number of players	14 (7x7)

Explanation

The white team tries to keep possession of the ball inside the square. The black team tries to steal the ball and, when it does, tries to get all of its players to touch the ball, while the white team will now press to try to avoid it.

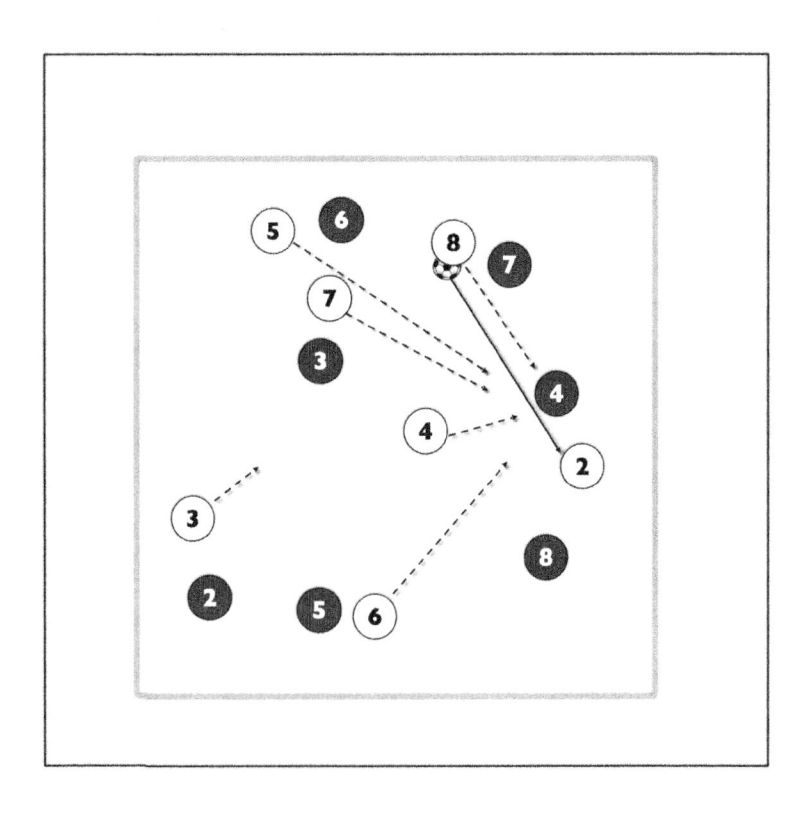

SOCCER: PRESSING JUST AFTER BALL LOSS

Drill 23	Main Objective	Improving pressing just after loss
	Number of players	14 (5+2x5+2)

Explanation

Players distributed as in the picture. Each team, when they have the ball, will have the support of their two wildcards on the outside. When they lose the ball, the team will press to recover the ball, entering the wild cards to press as well. And when they get the ball back, the wild cards will come out again to their starting position.

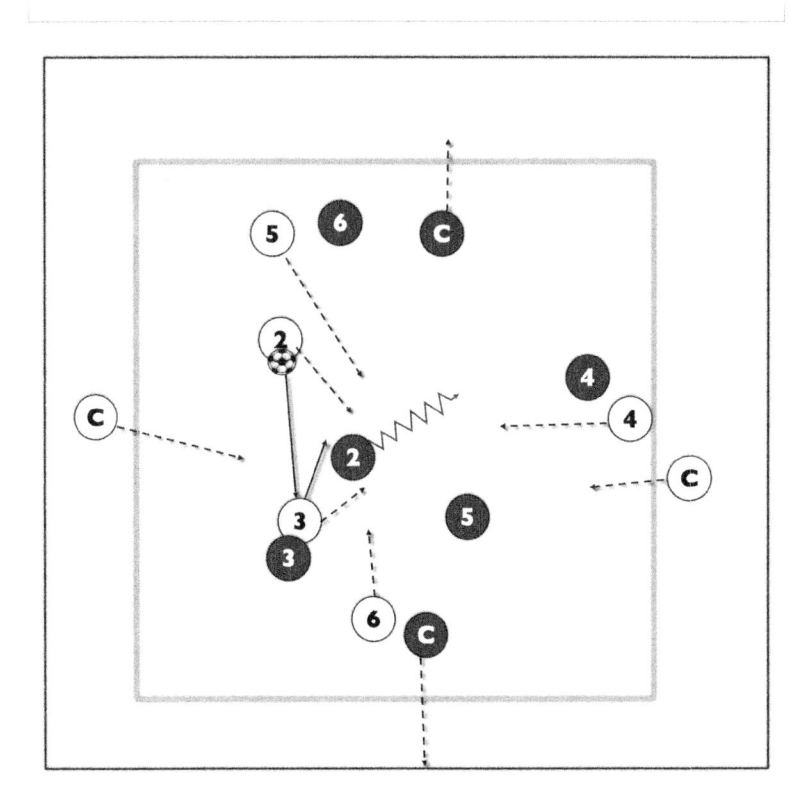

Ejercicio 24	Main Objective	Improving pressing just after loss
	Number of players	14 (7x7)

Explanation

The white team tries to keep possession of the ball within the major square. The black team tries to steal the ball and, when it does, the white team will try to keep the black team from putting the ball in the center square by pressing fast.

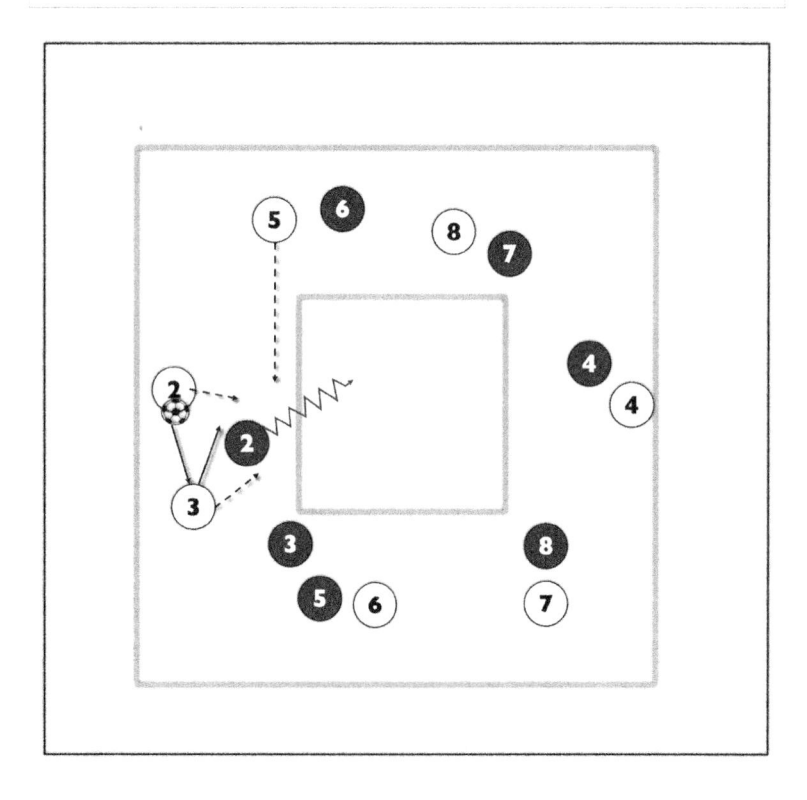

SOCCER: PRESSING JUST AFTER BALL LOSS

Drill 25	Main Objective	Improving pressing just after loss
	Number of players	12 (4x2+4x2)

Explanation

In a rectangle divided into two squares, players are placed 4x2, as in the layout of the image. The team that doesn't have the ball presses to steal it and, when it gets it, the last player to touch the ball and lost it, along with the player who stole the ball, will go to the other square to press and steal if their team doesn't have the ball, or to participate if their team has the ball. And so on.

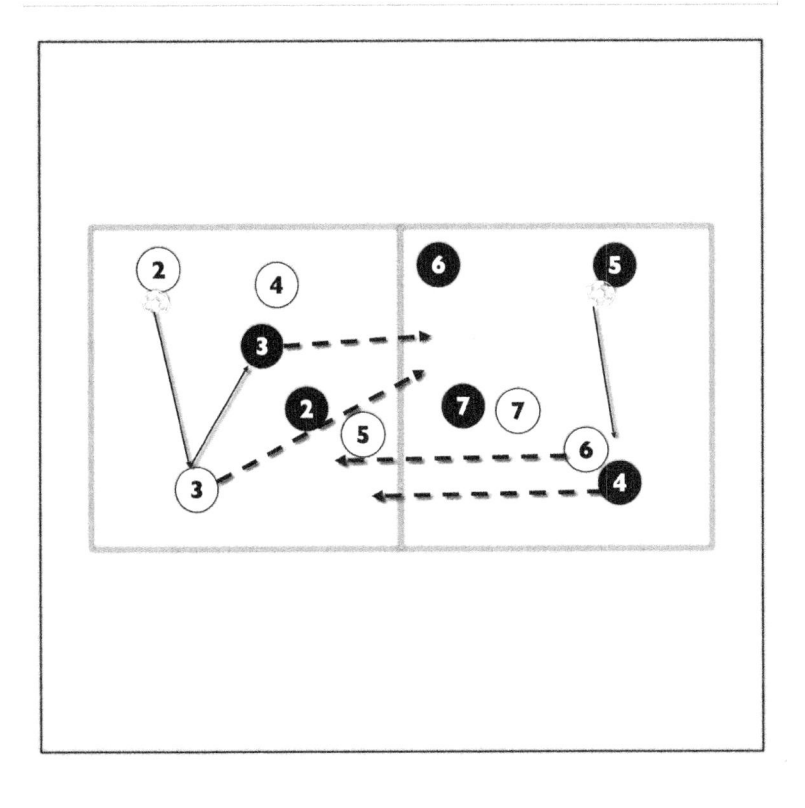

EDITORIAL WANCEULEN

Drill 26	Main Objective	Improving pressing just after loss
	Number of players	14 (7x7)

Explanation

The white team tries to keep possession of the ball within the major square. The black team tries to steal the ball and, when it does, the team that lost will press so that the other team does not play the ball with a teammate who will get into the small square to receive the ball.

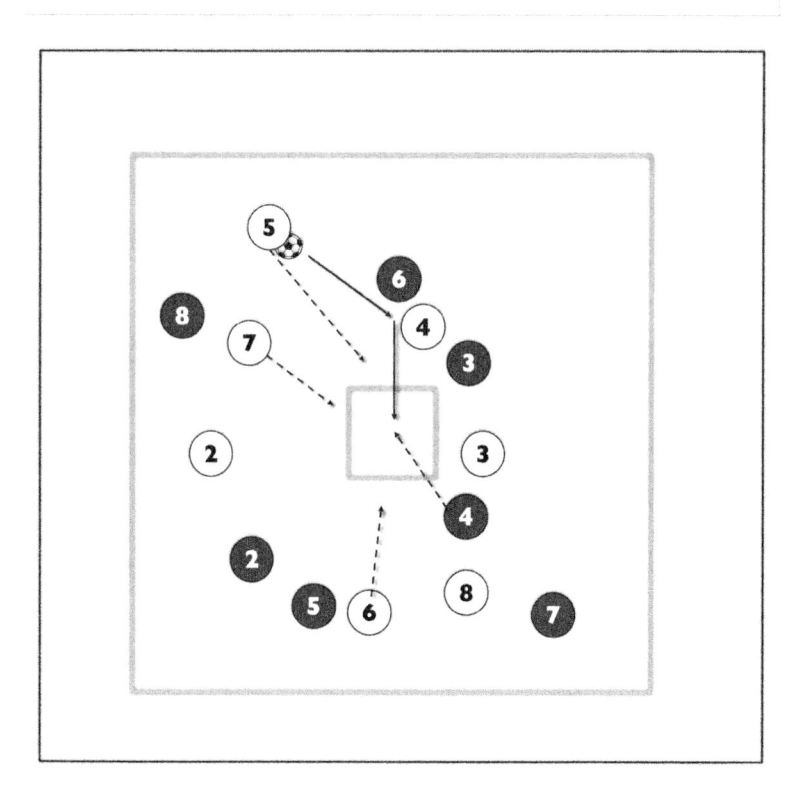

Drill 27	**Main Objective**	Improving pressing just after loss
	Number of players	10 (5x5)

Explanation

Players of the two teams, located as in the picture. The team that is on the outside with a player in the middle, passes the ball. When he loses it, they come to press until he recovers it and tries to get it out, and then keep passing it again.

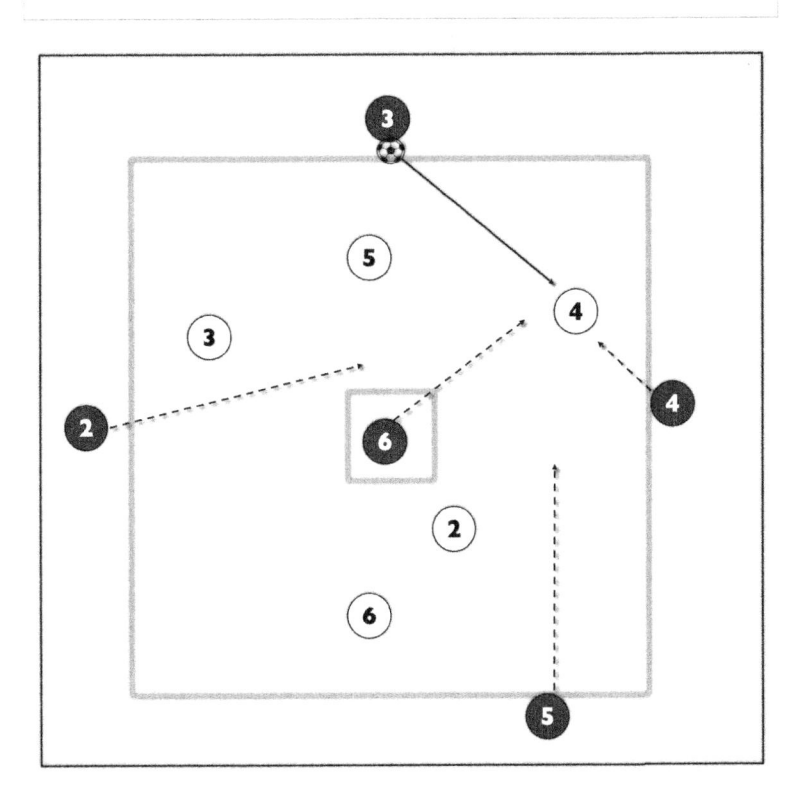

Drill 28	Main Objective	Improving pressing just after loss
	Number of players	8 (4x4)

Explanation

The players of the black team are each in a square. The white team are on the dividing lines passing the ball. When the black team recovers the ball, the white players will go to the player who has the ball to press and retrieve the ball.

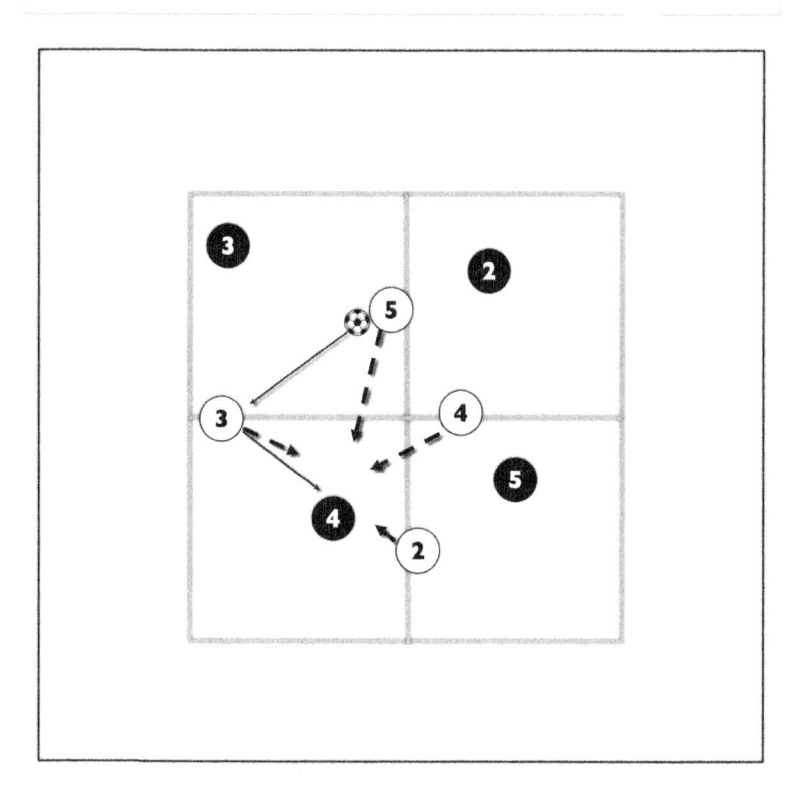

SOCCER: PRESSING JUST AFTER BALL LOSS

Drill 29	Main Objective	Improving pressing just after loss
	Number of players	8 (4x4)
	Explanation	

The players of the black team are each in a square. The white team are on the dividing lines passing the ball. When the black team loses the ball, it will press the white team, and when he recovers it, he will keep passing the ball.

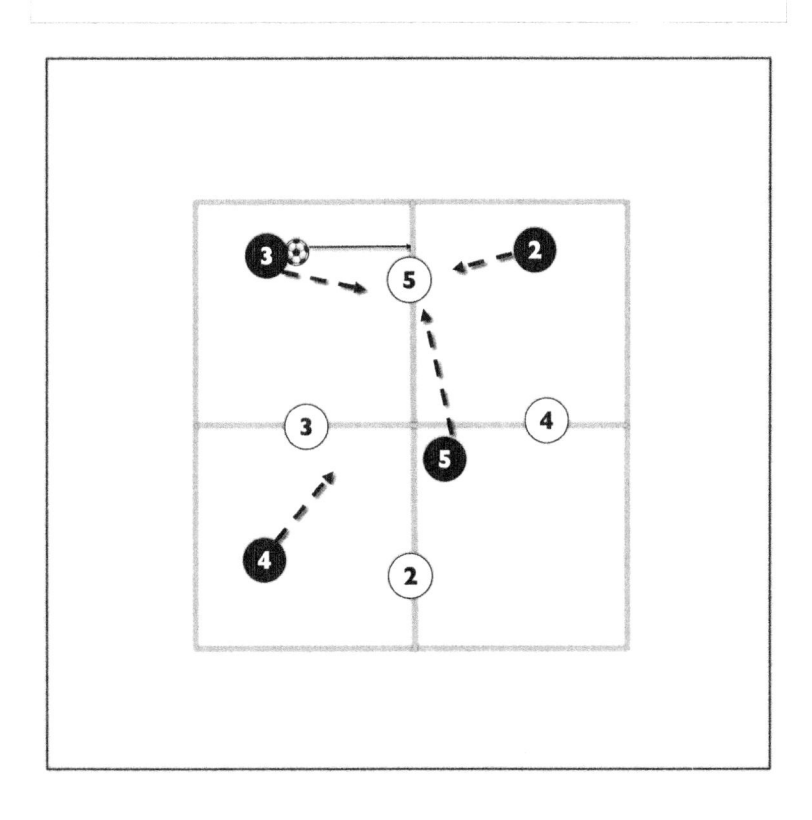

Drill 30	**Main Objective**	Improving pressing just after loss
	Number of players	10 (5x5)

Explanation

Players on the black team, with freedom of movement around the square, pass the ball. Those of the white team, on the dividing lines, will be able to intercept or anticipate. When the black team loses the ball it will press the white team (which will not be able to move from the lines), to try to recover the ball.

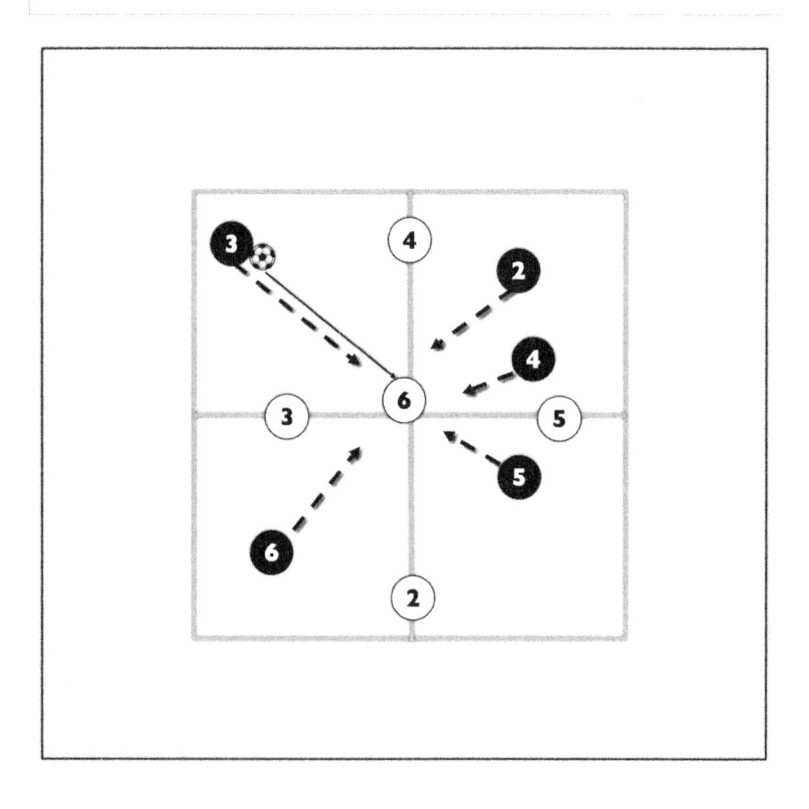

Drill 31	Main Objective	Improving pressing just after loss
	Number of players	18

Explanation

Inside the rectangle a team passes the ball. Another team tries to steal it. When a team loses the ball, the team that recovered it has to put each of its players without a ball in a small square. The team that lost the ball has to press the player who stole it to retrieve the ball, before the players of the other team enter all the small squares.

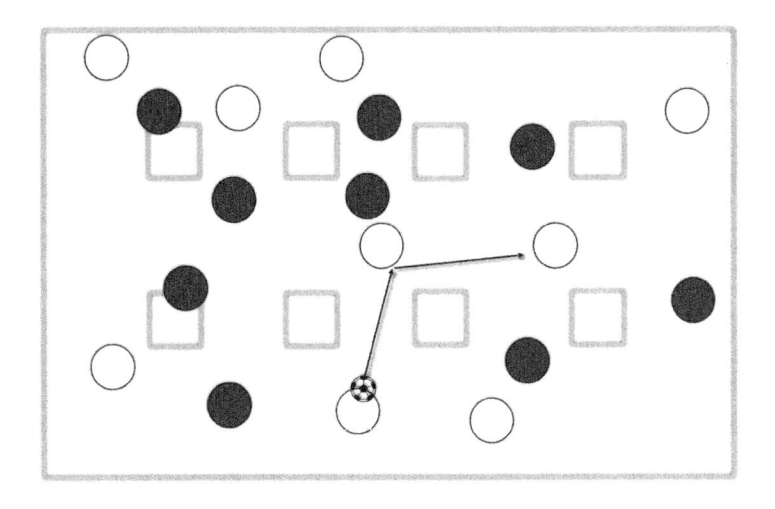

Drill 32	**Main Objective**	Improving pressing just after loss
	Number of players	19 (8x8+3)

Explanation

In a rectangle divided into 8 equal parts distributed players as in the image (2 in each square, one of each team) and wildcards over the lines. Each team will have to press the player who has the ball with the help of the wild cards. When one team loses the ball it moves to press the other with the help of the wildcards that can press from the lines that divide the rectangle.

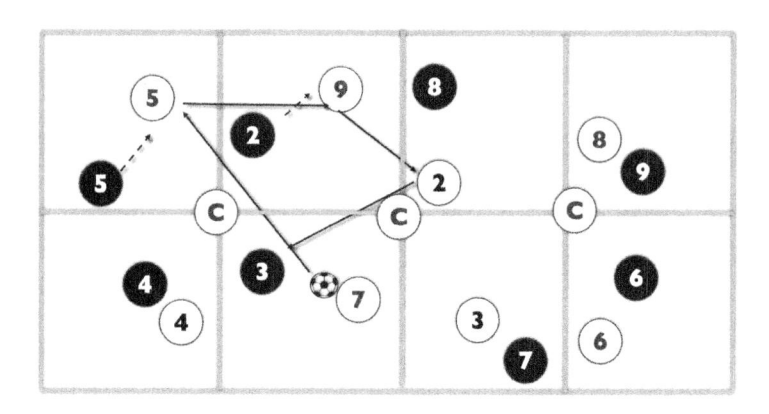

SOCCER: PRESSING JUST AFTER BALL LOSS

Drill 33	Main Objective	Improving pressing just after loss
	Number of players	22

Explanation

In the arrangement of the image. They pass 4x2 in each square (minus one that only passes the ball between them). When they steal the ball, the last two players who had touched the ball come out of the square, and go to the other square that had no opposing players. In that square that has been left with 4 players, they will pass the ball between them.

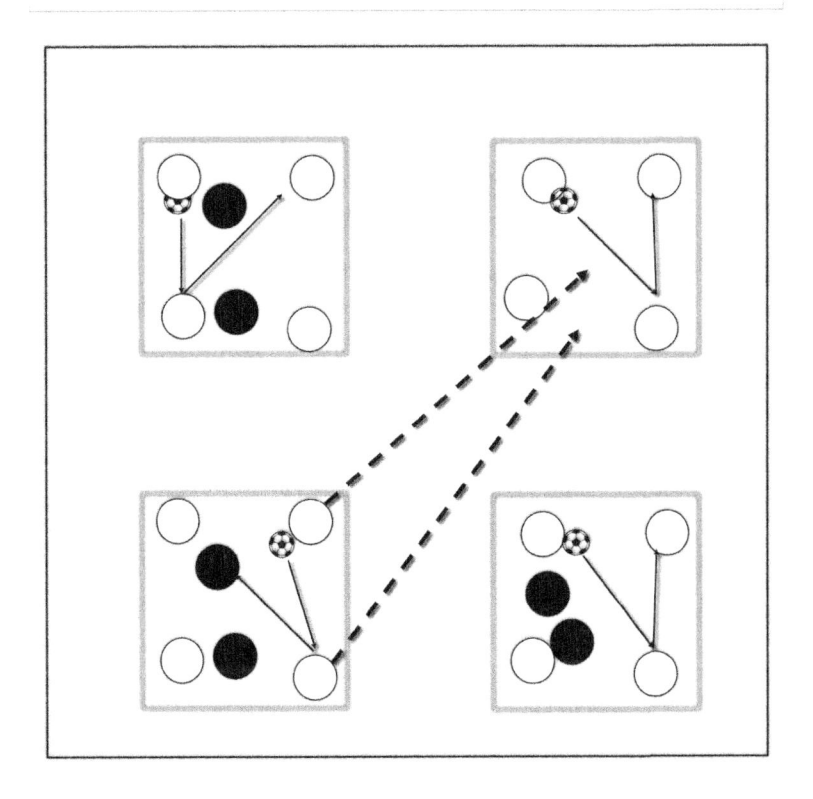

Drill 34	Main Objective	Improving pressing just after loss
	Number of players	11 (5x5+P)

Explanation

They will play 5x5 with a goalkeeper in an open goal (the goal is valid on both sides of the goal) inside the square. When one team recovers the ball, the team that lost it will press quickly to retrieve the ball, and to prevent the other team from scoring in the goal.

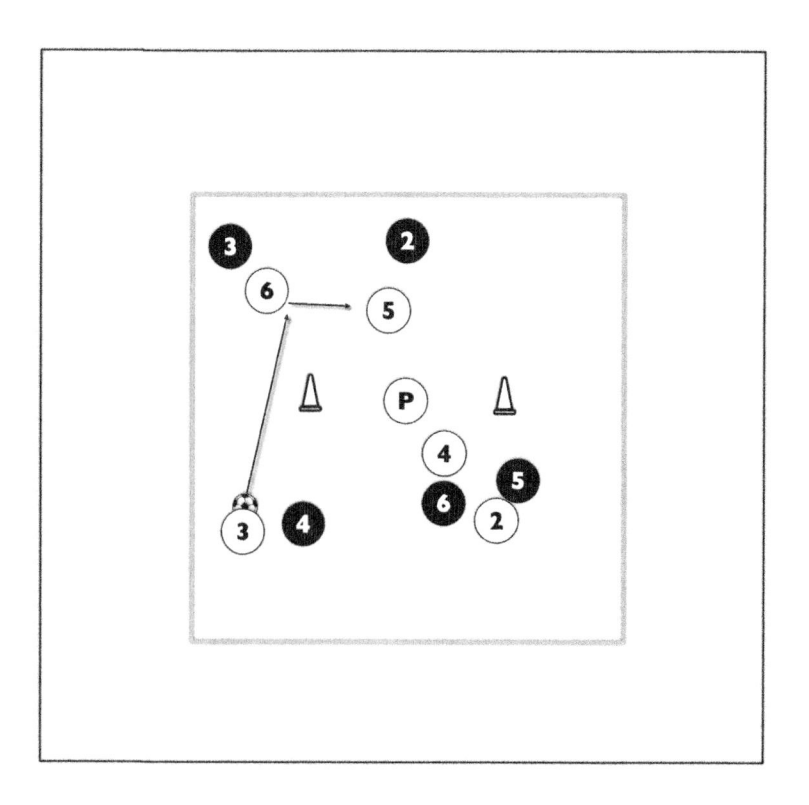

Drill 35	Main Objective	Improving pressing just after loss
	Number of players	10 (5x5)

Explanation

They will play 5x5, with 4 aisles to cross them driving the ball or through a pass. The team that loses the ball has to press the team that stole it, so that it does not cross the aisles.

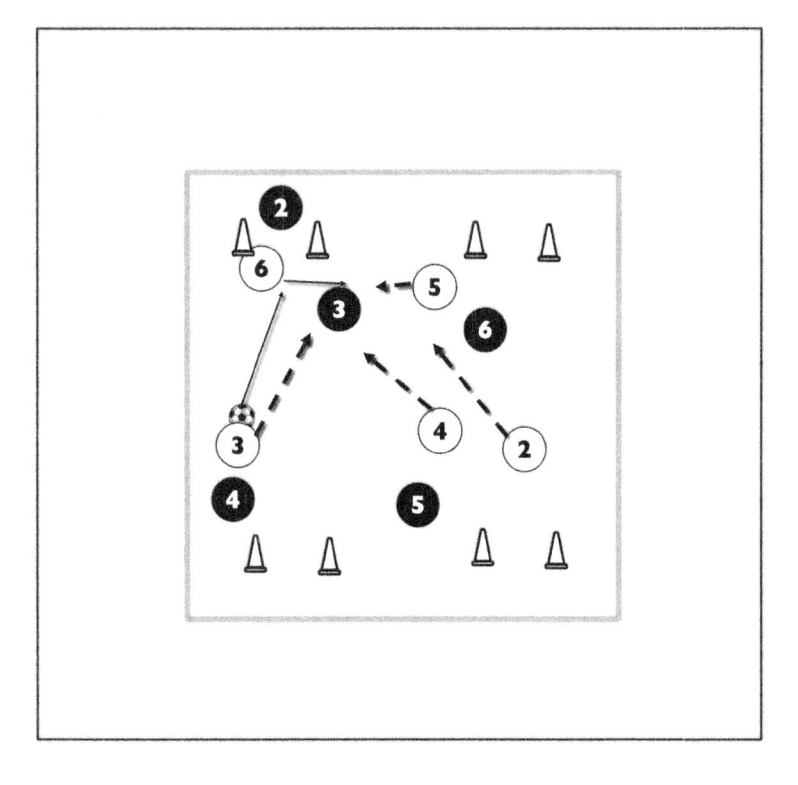

Drill 36	Main Objective	Improving pressing just after loss
	Number of players	6 (2x3+P)

Explanation

They play 2x3 placed according to the image. The two players on the white team press the number 4 player, and attempt to steal the ball when the number 3 player passes the ball to him. If the black team loses the ball, the white team's 2 players try to score, and black team players will press to avoid the goal.

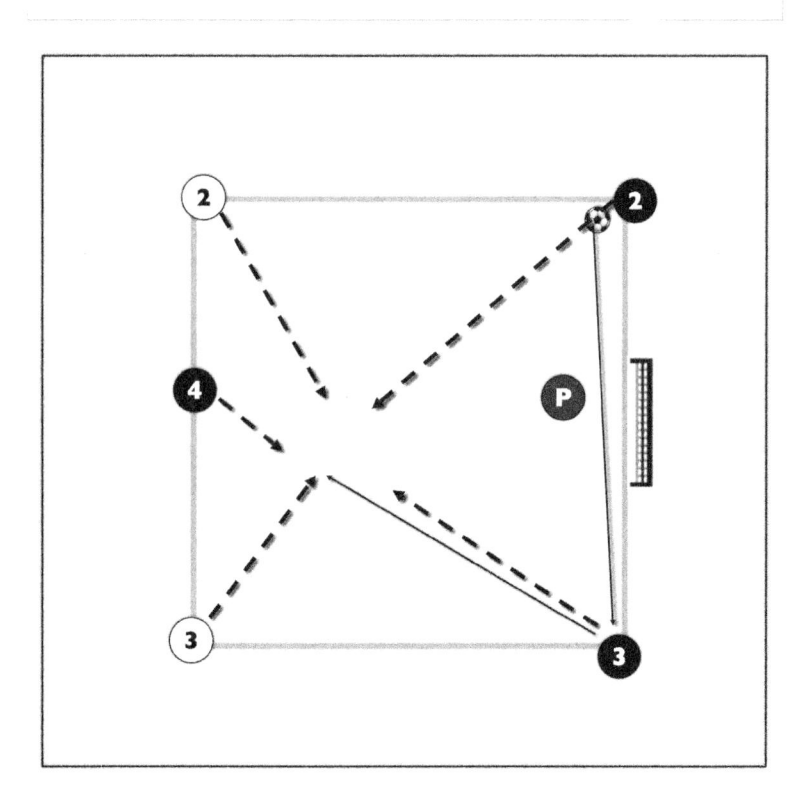

SOCCER: PRESSING JUST AFTER BALL LOSS

Drill 37	Main Objective	Improving pressing just after loss
	Number of players	6 (2x3+P)

Explanation

Players placed as in the picture, the goalkeeper pulls any of the players out of the white team and the black team presses so that they cannot score.

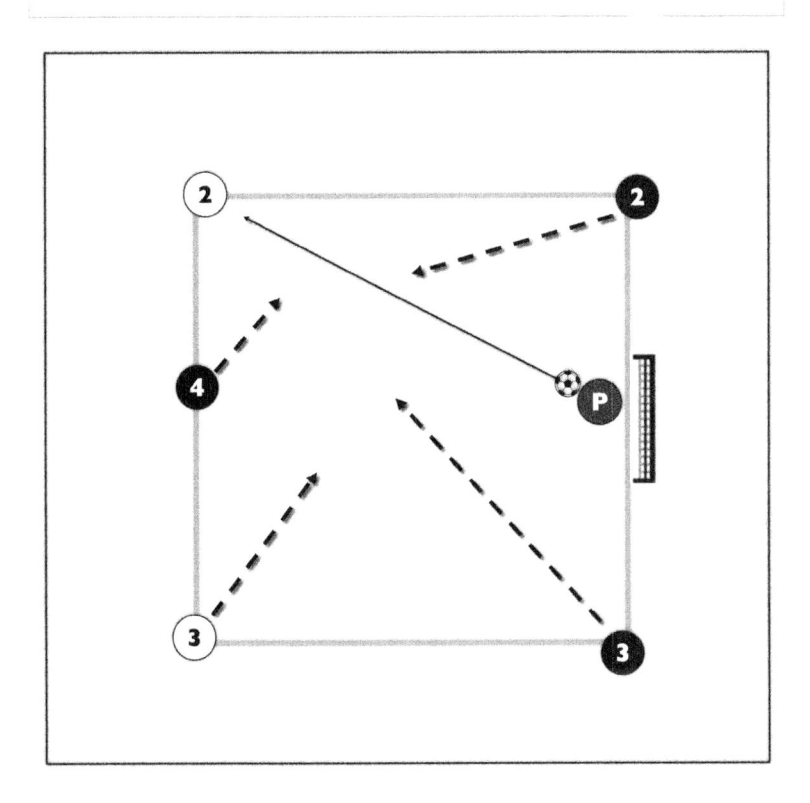

Drill 38	Main Objective	Improving pressing just after loss
	Number of players	11 (5x5+P)

Explanation

5x5 with a goalkeeper. When a team recovers the ball, the team that lost will press quickly to recover the ball so that the opponent cannot score.

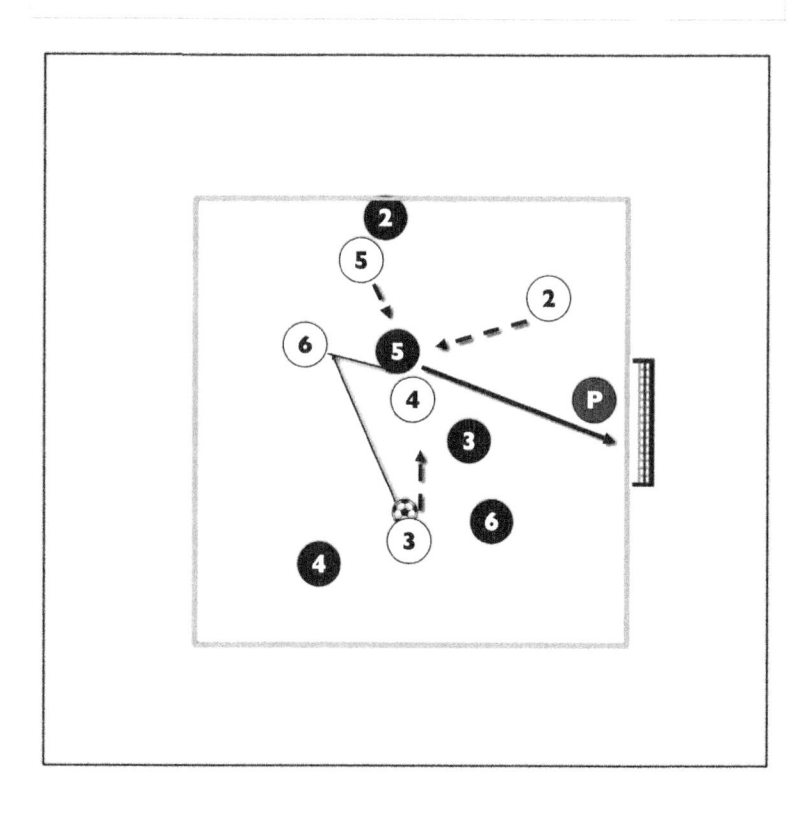

SOCCER: PRESSING JUST AFTER BALL LOSS

Drill 39	Main Objective	Improving pressing just after loss
	Number of players	9 (4x4+P)

Explanation

Players are placed according to the arrangement of the image. The white team maintains possession of the ball. The black team tries to steal the ball and take it to the other half and score. The white team, when the ball loses, will press to recover it quickly so that the opponent cannot go to the other square and throw to the goal.

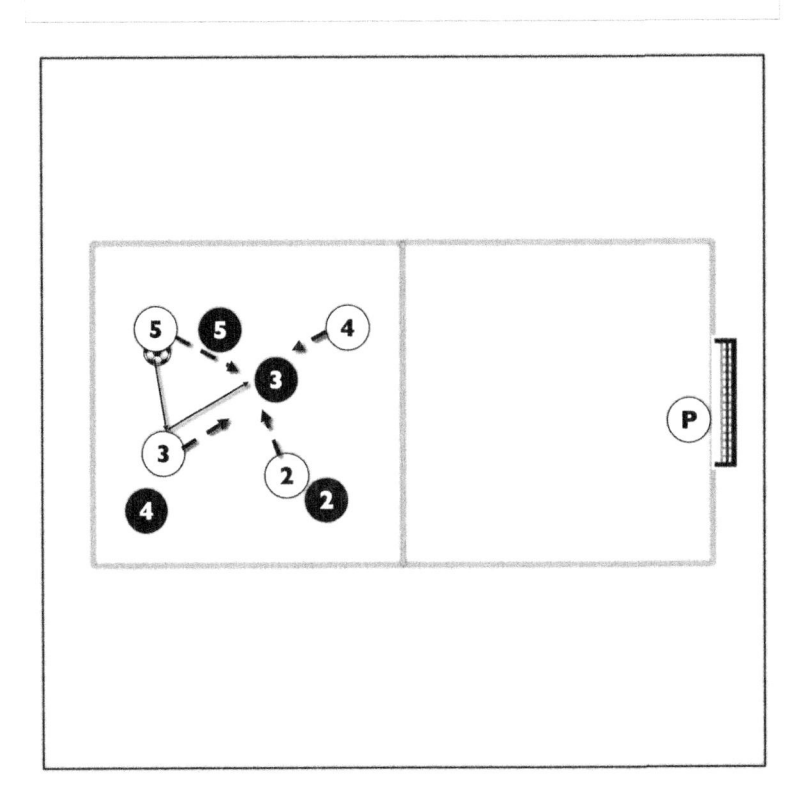

Drill	Main Objective	Improving pressing just after loss
40	Number of players	10 (3x3x3+P)

Explanation

Three teams of three players each. One team attacks another, as in the picture. The third team, wait in the middle line. If the first team shoots at goal, or the ball comes out, or if the other team recovers it, the ball is taken by the third team in the middle, and the same action is repeated.

The defending team goes to the middle line, and the team that has attacked, is now the defending team.

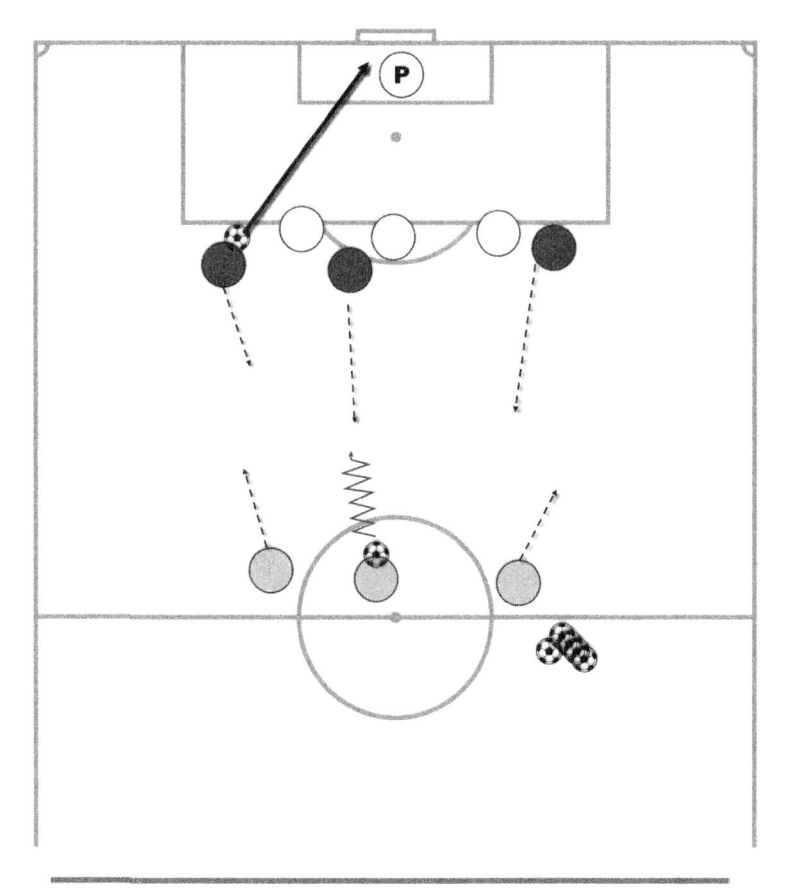

SOCCER: PRESSING JUST AFTER BALL LOSS

Drill 42	Main Objective	Improving pressing just after loss
	Number of players	6 (2x3+P)
	Explanation	

Players placed as in the picture. The black team passes the ball to the white team. The white team attacks the opposing goal. The black team comes out to press so that the white team does not get a goal. If the white team loses the ball, press the black team to not score on the other goal.

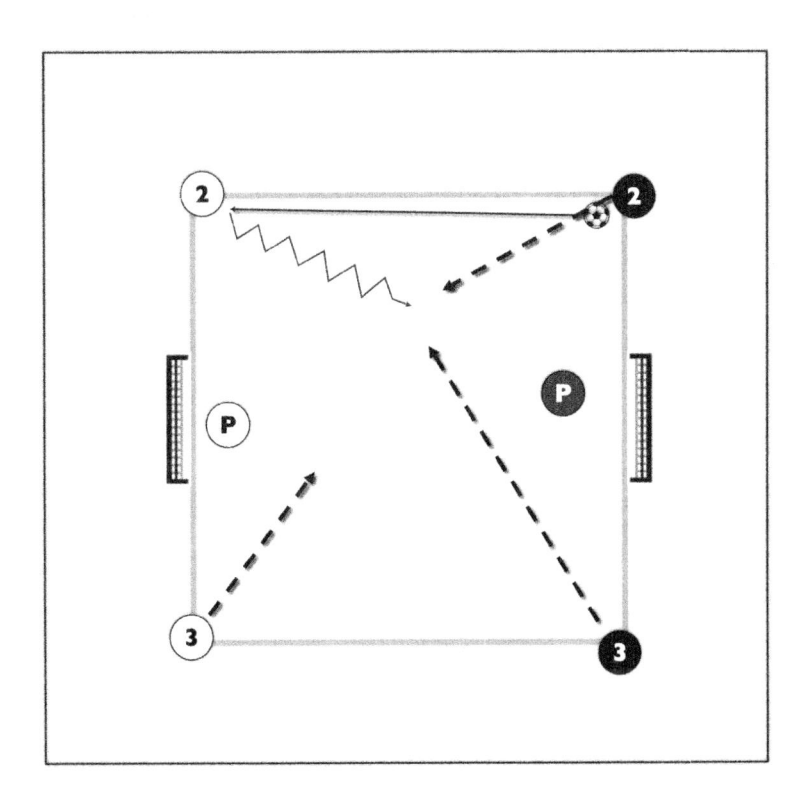

Drill 42	Main Objective	Improving pressing just after loss
	Number of players	10 (4+Px4+P)

Explanation

Players are placed according to the arrangement of the image. The white team has the ball and tries to score a goal. The black team tries to remove the ball from the white team so that it does not score and take the ball to the other half. The white team, when he loses the ball, presses to recover quickly and score.

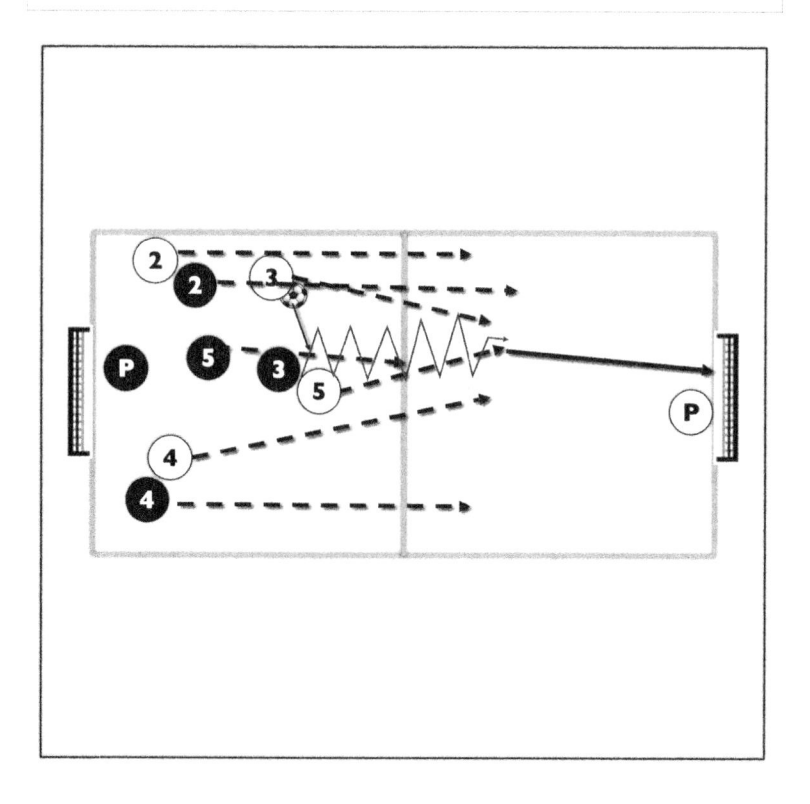

SOCCER: PRESSING JUST AFTER BALL LOSS

Drill 43	Main Objective	Improving pressing just after loss
	Number of players	(P+3x1+P+2)

Explanation

3 attackers and 1 defender. 2 players wait on the baseline. When attackers shoot at goal or lose the ball, the two players in the background go out to accompany the one who was alone and the three attack opposite goal. The three who attacked will press to recover the ball. Rotate roles.

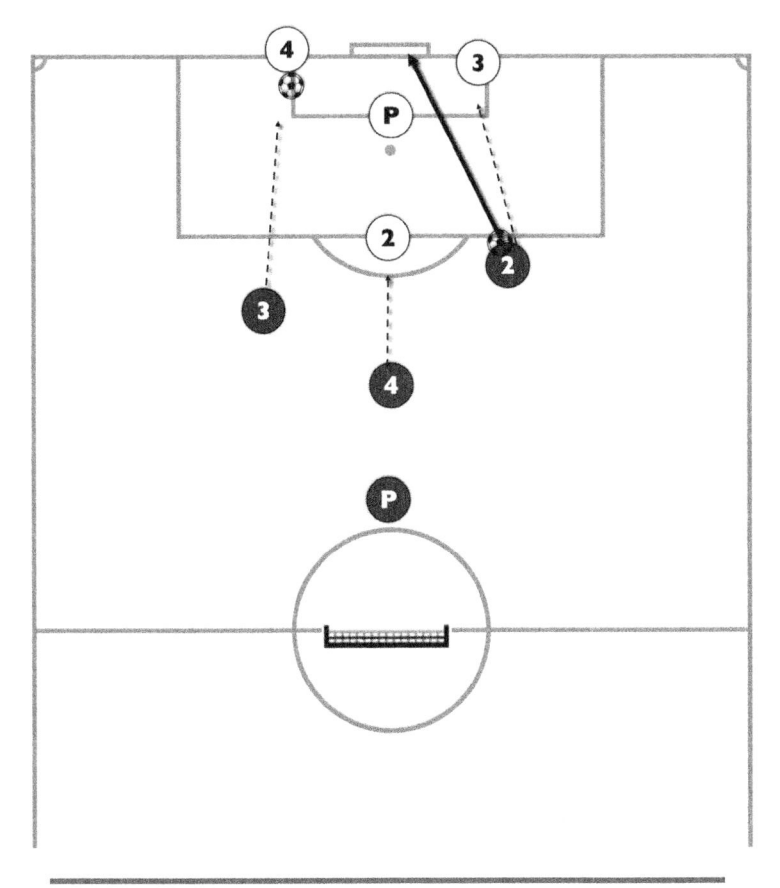

EDITORIAL WANCEULEN

Drill 44	Main Objective	Improving pressing just after loss
	Number of players	20 (7+Px7+4+P)

Explanation

Players are placed according to the arrangement of the image. El equipo que inicia el juego, junto con los comodines (que sólo se moverán como apoyos en las líneas de banda) cada vez que pierda el balón presionarán (junto con los comodines) para recuperar hasta que se consiga un gol o salga el balón. Cuando esto pase, atacará el otro equipo con la ayuda de los comodines y para la presión cuando lo pierdan.

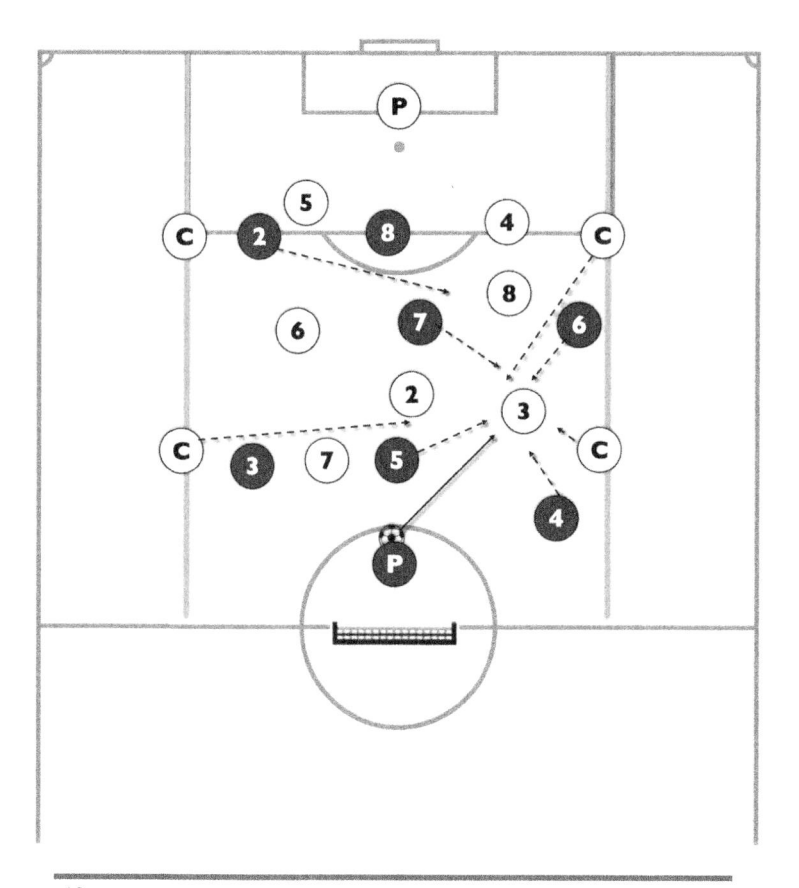

SOCCER: PRESSING JUST AFTER BALL LOSS

Drill 45	Main Objective	Improving pressing just after loss
	Number of players	22 (8+2+Px8+2+P)

Explanation

In middle line, with two side aisles, teams will place one player in each side aisle who will not participate when they have the ball. When a team loses the ball, the players on their team who were in the corridors will come to press and when they recover it they will return to their aisles.

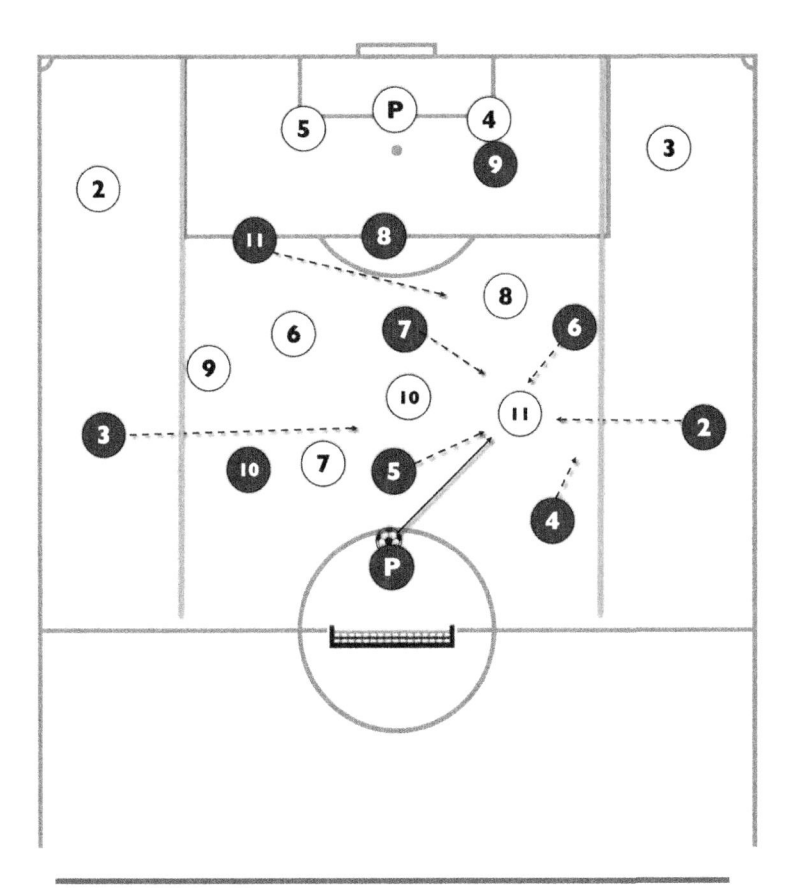

Drill 46	Main Objective	Improving pressing just after loss
	Number of players	22 (10+Px10+P)

Explanation

Match in which the two teams will press high the exit of the opposing team, and the team that has the ball, when it loses it at the start of the game, will press fast to recover it.

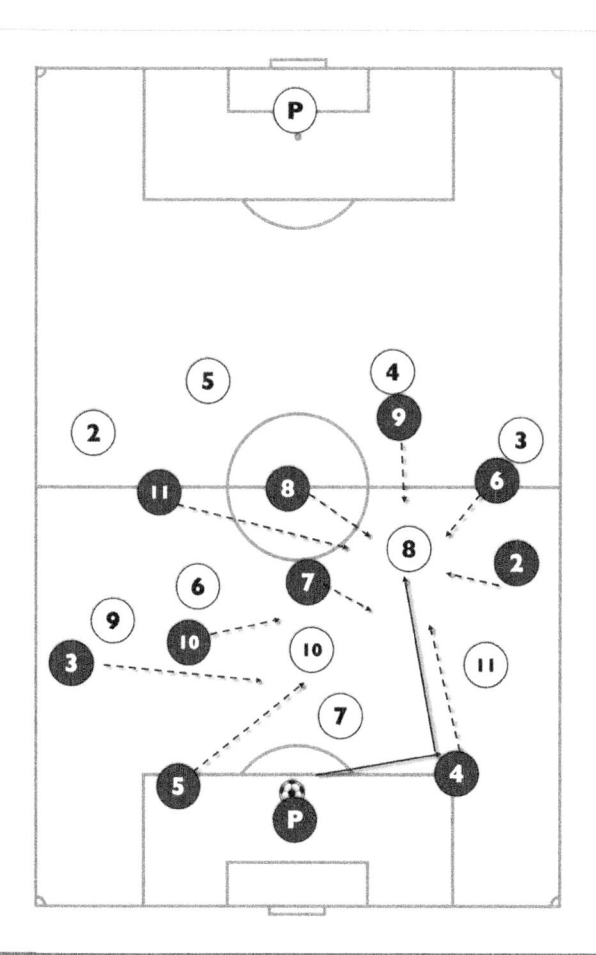

SOCCER: PRESSING JUST AFTER BALL LOSS

Drill 47	Main Objective	Improving pressing just after loss
	Number of players	22 (10+Px10+P)
	Explanation	

Match in which the two teams will press the opposing team with one to one defense across the field each time a ball loss occurs.

Drill 48	Main Objective	Improving pressing just after loss
	Number of players	22 (10+Px10+P)

Explanation

Match in which the two teams will place all their players, except the goalkeeper, on the field where the ball is at every moment, to press when there is a loss. If a team scores a goal and that team is not fully on the field where the ball is, the goal will be voided. If a team receives a goal and the team is not fully on the field where the ball is, the goal will be worth double.

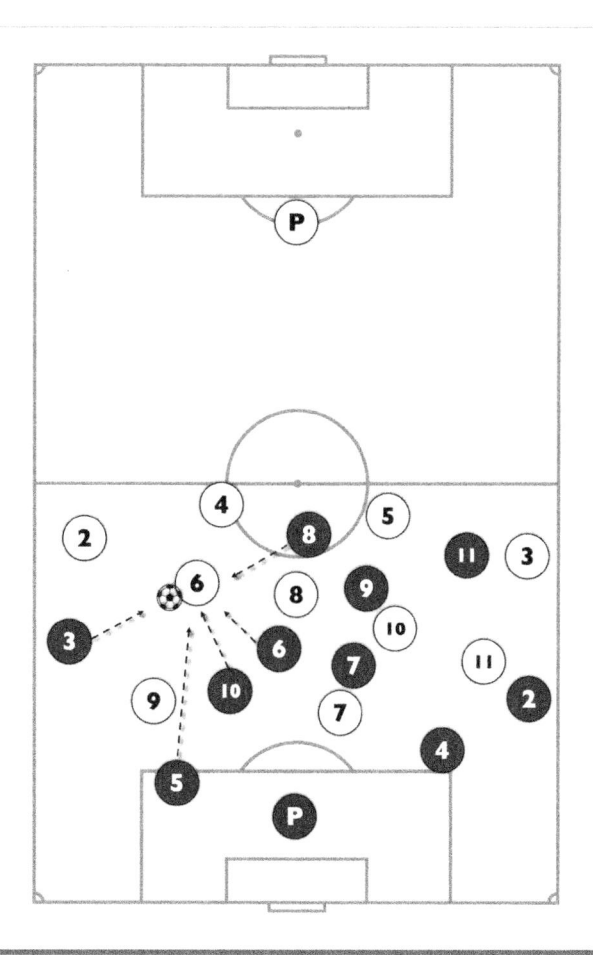

SOCCER: PRESSING JUST AFTER BALL LOSS

Drill 49	Main Objective	Improving pressing just after loss
	Number of players	22 (9+Px9+2+P)

Explanation

Playing a match with two wildcards, who will help put pressure on the teams when they lose the ball. When a team retrieves the ball, the wild cards will help the other team press.

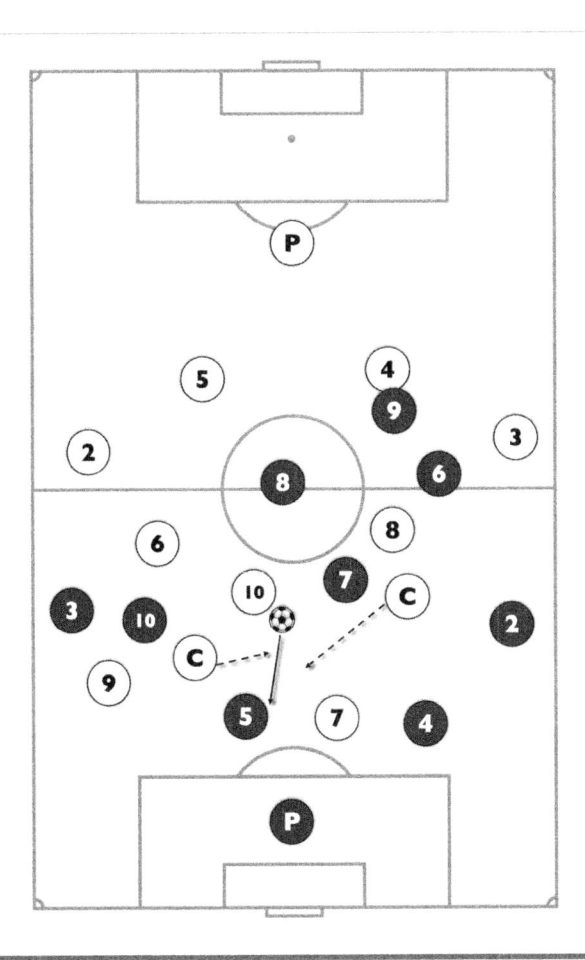

EDITORIAL WANCEULEN

Drill 50	**Main Objective**	Improving pressing just after loss
	Number of players	22 (9+Px9+2+P)

Explanation

Playing a match. Each time a team loses the ball, the player who loses the ball and the two closest, will press quickly to recover the ball, until they can recover it.

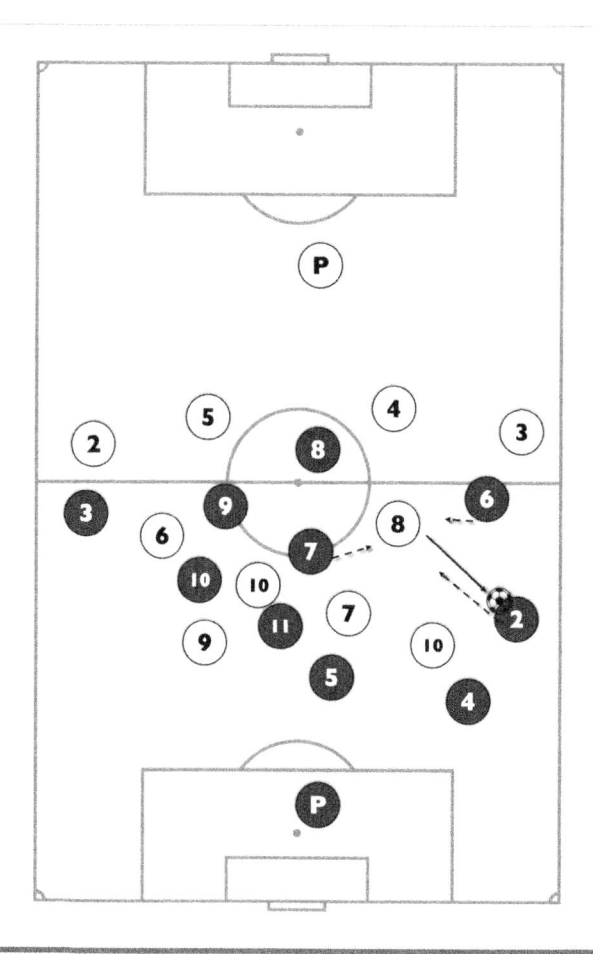

BIBLIOGRAPHY

- Couto, A. (2015): *Las grandes escuelas del Fútbol Moderno.* Editorial Fútbol de libro.
- Castellano, Julen y Casamichana, David (2016): *El arte de planificar en fútbol,* Editorial Futbol de libro.
- Castellano, Julen; Casamichana, David y San Román, Jaime (2015): *Los juegos reducidos en el entrenamiento del fútbol.* Editorial Futbol de libro.
- Cano Moreno, Oscar (2010): *Fútbol: Entrenamiento global basado en la interpretación del juego.* Editorial Wanceulen.
- López López, Javier (2009): *500 juegos para el entrenamiento físico con balón.* Editorial Wanceulen.
- López López, Javier (2009): *400 tareas integradas para el entrenamiento de la táctica ofensiva.* Editorial Wanceulen.
- López López, Javier; Wanceulen Moreno, Antonio; Wanceulen Moreno, José F. y Bernal Ruiz, Javier (2009): *225 juegos para el entrenamiento integrado del pase en el fútbol.* Editorial Wanceulen.
- González, Alberto (2013): *Fútbol. Dinámica del juego desde la perspectiva de las transiciones.* Editorial Learning 11.
- Fradua, Luis (1997): *La visión periférica del futbolista.* Editorial Paidotribo.
- Mayer, R. (1996): *Fichas de fútbol. 120 juegos de ataque y defensa.* Hispano Europea. Barcelona.
- Garganta, J. y Pinto, J. en Graça, A. y Oliveira, J. (1997): *La enseñanza de los juegos Deportivos.* Editorial Paidotribo.
- Castelo, J. (1999): *Futbol. Estructura y dinámica del juego.* Editorial INDE. Barcelona.
- Caneda, R. (1999): *La zona en Fútbol.* Editorial Wanceulen. Sevilla.
- Seirul´lo, F. (1999): *Criterios modernos del entrenamiento en el fútbol.* Revista Training Fútbol. Valladolid.

- García Ocaña, Francisco (2008): *Fútbol y Fútbol sala: 250 actividades sociomotrices.* Editorial Paidotribo. Barcelona.
- López López, Javier (2013): *Fútbol: Senior (2013): 175 fichas de sesiones de entrenamiento.* Editorial Wanceulen. Sevilla.
- López López, Javier (2013): *Fútbol: Juveniles: 160 fichas de sesiones de entrenamiento.* Editorial Wanceulen. Sevilla.
- López López, Javier (2009): Fútbol: *1380 Juegos globales para el aprendizaje y perfeccionamiento de la técnica ofensiva y defensiva.* Editorial Wanceulen. Sevilla.
- López López, Javier (2008): *Fútbol: Cadetes: 160 fichas de sesiones de entrenamiento.* Editorial Wanceulen. Sevilla.
- López López, Javier (2013): *Fútbol: Infantiles: 120 fichas de sesiones de entrenamiento.* Editorial Wanceulen. Sevilla.
- López López, Javier (2008): *Fútbol: Alevines: 120 fichas de sesiones de entrenamiento.* Editorial Wanceulen. Sevilla.
- López López, Javier (2013): *Fútbol: Benjamines: 80 fichas de sesiones de entrenamiento.* Editorial Wanceulen. Sevilla.
- López López, Javier (2009): *Fútbol: Prebenjamines: 80 fichas de sesiones de entrenamiento.* Editorial Wanceulen. Sevilla.

Printed in Great Britain
by Amazon